W9-AWQ-369

THEY SHOT
THE
PRESIDENT

Ten True Stories

Other Scholastic paperbacks you will enjoy:

Disaster! The Destruction of Our Planet
by George Sullivan

Medical Mysteries: Six Deadly Cases
by Dian Dincin Buchman

Mr. President: A Book of U.S. Presidents
by George Sullivan

Great Escapes of World War II
by George Sullivan

The Assassinations of John and Robert Kennedy
by Leroy Hayman

THEY SHOT THE PRESIDENT

Ten True Stories
by George Sullivan

SCHOLASTIC INC.
New York Toronto London Auckland Sydney

Picture Credits

Cover: Top, UPI/Bettmann. Right, AP/Wide World. Bottom, Michael Evans, The White House.

Interior: Pages 5, 10, 36, and 68, New York Public Library. Page 14, National Portrait Gallery. Page 16, National Park Service. Pages 23 and 29, *Harper's Weekly*. Pages 32, 50, and 71, Library of Congress. Pages 33, 46, 65, 103, 114, 116, 129, 136, 144, 156 (top), 157, 159, 163, 164, 172, 177, and 179, AP/Wide World. Page 38, the collection of Sal Alberti. Page 52, George Sullivan. Pages 54, 57, and 66, Buffalo and Erie County Historical Society. Pages 74, 81, and 82, Theodore Roosevelt Collection, Harvard College Library. Page 83, Milwaukee County Historical Society. Pages 87, 89, 95, and 98, Franklin D. Roosevelt Library. Pages 96 and 134, UPI/Bettmann. Page 112, Harry S Truman Library. Page 120, Golden West Television. Page 122, Assassination Archives & Research Center. Pages 142 and 175, *The New York Times*. Page 156 (bottom), Gerald R. Ford Library. Page 169, *Movie Star News*. Page 173, Michael Evans, The White House.

If you purchased this book without a cover, you should be aware that this book is stolen property. It was reported as "unsold and destroyed" to the publisher, and neither the author nor the publisher has received any payment for this "stripped book."

No part of this publication may be reproduced in whole or in part, or stored in a retrieval system, or transmitted in any form or by any means, electronic, mechanical, photocopying, recording, or otherwise, without written permission of the publisher. For information regarding permission, write to Scholastic Inc., 730 Broadway, New York, NY 10003.

ISBN 0-590-46101-X

Copyright © 1993 by George Sullivan.
All rights reserved. Published by Scholastic Inc.
APPLE PAPERBACKS® is a registered trademark of Scholastic Inc.

12   11   10   9   8   7   6   5   4   3   6   7   8/9

Printed in the U.S.A.   40

First Scholastic printing, November 1993

THEY SHOT THE PRESIDENT

Ten True Stories

Introduction

Early in the afternoon of November 1, 1950, President Harry Truman, taking a nap in Blair House, across Pennsylvania Avenue from the White House (which was under repair), was abruptly awakened by shots outside. Two gunmen were shooting it out with Secret Service agents and police officers in a reckless attempt to get inside and assassinate him. The fierce struggle ended with Truman safe, but two men were fatally shot and three wounded.

Truman, shrugging off the incident, carried out his schedule of activities that afternoon. He said, "A president has to expect those things."

Sadly, it is true.

Ten of the forty-two American presidents have

been victims of assassination attempts. Four times the attempts have proven fatal — in the case of Abraham Lincoln in 1865, James Garfield (1881), William McKinley (1901), and John F. Kennedy (1963).

The word "assassin" is Arabic in origin. It comes from *hashshashin*, meaning a member of an ancient terrorist sect who killed their political enemies while under the influence of hashish, the flowering tops or leaves of Indian hemp. A person who smokes, chews, or drinks hashish achieves a kind of a drunken state, becomes stoned, zonked, or freaked out.

But those words do not describe American assassins. They have not been drug abusers. They have been clear-headed when they acted (or at least their thinking at the time was not influenced by chemicals).

There are exceptions, of course, but most American assassins or would-be assassins have been drifters and loners. Frustrated and confused, they have led lives apart from society. They are misfits, often with some wrong they are seeking to make right. Killing the president, they feel, will make everything okay.

In Japan, assassins frequently use knives. In the Middle East, the hand grenade is not uncommon. Not here; Americans prefer guns. In every attempt on a President's life, a pistol or rifle has been used.

Handguns are a particular problem. A handgun

can be concealed in a pocket, stuffed in the belt, or stashed in one's purse. Stricter controls on handguns might reduce the ease with which a president or other public officials can be attacked.

Every president receives threats against his life. No matter how great the security, being president will always be a risky business. In 1968, following the shooting death of black civil rights leader Martin Luther King, Robert Kennedy, brother of the murdered president, said: "And yet it goes on, and on, and on . . . why?" Several weeks later, Kennedy himself was gunned down by a lunatic assassin.

1
"King Richard"

Andrew Jackson, the seventh president, was the first to be born in a log cabin and the first to fight a duel. He was also the first president to be the victim of an assassination attempt.

The attack took place in the Capitol on January 30, 1835. The sixty-seven-year-old president, white-haired and frail, was in his second term.

Earlier in the month, on January 8, Jackson's friends had given a lavish banquet on his behalf. The date was the anniversary of the Battle of New Orleans, Jackson's stirring triumph over the British in the War of 1812. The victory helped to make Jackson, an Army major general at the time, a national hero.

A second reason for the dinner was to celebrate

Andrew Jackson, the seventh president, was the first to be an assassin's target.

the final payment on the national debt. Jackson was the first and only president to preside over a debtless government.

On the cold gray morning of January 30, the president left the White House for the Capitol to attend a funeral service for Warren R. Davis, a congressman from South Carolina. The service was to be held in the assembly chamber of the House of Representatives, a large, semicircular room south of the rotunda.

As the president entered the Capitol and crossed the rotunda, he was watched by the trim and handsome Richard Lawrence, a crazed Washington house painter. Throughout much of his adult life, Lawrence had displayed bizarre behavior. The attack he planned on President Jackson was simply one more example.

Born in England in 1800 or 1801, Richard Lawrence was brought to the United States at the age of twelve. His family settled in the Washington area and he lived what seems to have been a quite normal and uneventful life, at least for a time. Relatives and acquaintances were later to describe Richard Lawrence as "a remarkably fine boy" and "one of good moral habits."

When he was old enough to earn a living, Lawrence decided he wanted to be a house painter. He became a skilled and steady worker. As a hobby, he enjoyed landscape painting.

A few years before the murder attempt at the Capitol, Lawrence's family began to notice a worrisome change in his behavior. Lawrence started feeling threatened by others and was subject to fits of rage and wild laughter. Sometimes he went about talking to himself. He lost interest in his work.

Richard Lawrence explained to his bewildered sister that he did not need to work anymore because the United States government owed him enormous sums of money, millions of dollars. His case was now before Congress, he said. His claim was based on the belief that he was, in fact, King Richard III of England.

He further believed that President Jackson was disputing his demands. Were Jackson to be removed, Lawrence felt, the vice president would surely recognize his claims to be valid.

Boys in the neighborhood who heard this tale began calling him "King Richard." It was a nickname Richard Lawrence liked.

Besides having these delusions, Lawrence sometimes behaved violently. He once threatened to kill a black maid because he claimed she was laughing at him. Another time, he frightened his sister by threatening to strike her with a paperweight because he thought she had been talking about him.

In the rooming house where he lived, Lawrence ran up a big bill, then announced he had no intention of paying it until he received the money that Congress owed him. When his landlady insisted he pay, Lawrence threatened to cut her throat or blow her brains out. He also refused to pay other bills.

In the weeks preceding his assault upon the president, Richard Lawrence would often sit in his paint shop talking to himself. Jackson was seldom far from his thoughts. "Damn General Jackson!" he kept saying. "Damn him; he does not know his enemy!"

On the morning of the day of the attack, Lawrence was seen sitting on a chest in his paint shop.

7

He was holding a book and laughing loudly. He suddenly tossed the book aside and declared, "I'll be damned if I don't do it!" With that, Richard Lawrence arose, put a pair of single-shot pistols into his pockets, draped a cloak over his shoulders, and set off for the Capitol. He knew a funeral service for Congressman Davis was being held at noon, and President Jackson would be there.

When he arrived at the Capitol, it did not take Richard Lawrence long to find where the funeral service was being held. As he stalked the president, Lawrence clutched a pistol in each hand beneath his cloak. Several days before, he had loaded them carefully, using lead balls of just the right size and gunpowder of the highest quality. He knew the pistols would be able to do what he wanted, because he had fired one of them through a wooden plank an inch thick.

Richard Lawrence riveted his eyes on the stooped figure of the president as he and members of his cabinet took their seats among the mourners. Lawrence had made no attempt to shoot the president when he arrived, because, as he was to explain later, he did not wish to disrupt the funeral.

The service lasted about an hour. Before it ended, Richard Lawrence left his post to cross back through the rotunda and out onto the East Portico, a kind of spacious porch that led to the Capitol's main entrance. The East Portico is where presidential inaugurations have often been held. In 1835, its appearance was much the same as it is today.

When the service was over, the mourners joined in a procession that led out of the assembly chamber through the rotunda and to the door leading to the East Portico. The president, walking with a cane and leaning on the arm of Levi Woodbury, the secretary of the treasury, took his place in the line. Lawrence, meanwhile, having cocked the pistols, slipped in behind one of the portico's massive pillars and waited for the president to appear.

It was a short wait. When the president made his way out onto the portico, Richard Lawrence flung aside his cloak, stepped forward, aimed the pistol in his right hand at Jackson's heart, and squeezed the trigger. The percussion cap that was meant to light the powder exploded as it was supposed to, but it did not ignite the powder, and the gun did not fire.

As many of those around Jackson panicked, Richard Lawrence remained calm. He dropped the first pistol and shifted the second from his left hand to his right, then aimed at the president again. By now, the president was charging at Lawrence with his cane upraised. When Lawrence pulled the trigger, the second pistol, incredibly, also misfired.

All was bedlam. Several men from the funeral procession lunged at Lawrence and quickly subdued him. Although he had failed in his mission,

As Richard Lawrence takes aim at Jackson, the president's aides react in horror.

Richard Lawrence won a place in history as the first person to make an attempt upon the life of a United States president.

At his trial following the assassination attempt, Lawrence pleaded insanity as his defense. He had plenty of witnesses to testify to his lunatic behavior. It took the jury only five minutes to decide that he was not criminally responsible for his act.

Richard Lawrence spent the rest of his life in prisons and mental hospitals. He died at the Government Hospital for the Insane in Washington (now St. Elizabeth's Hospital) in 1861, sixteen years after the death of Jackson.

No one could ever say for certain why both of Lawrence's pistols had misfired on that fateful day. A Washington newspaper claimed that the chance of a misfire of a single pistol was one in 125,000. For two pistols, the odds were astronomical.

It was determined that the two pistols had been loaded correctly and that Richard Lawrence had fired them many times without anything going wrong. Lawrence told police he believed they had misfired because the day's humid weather conditions had dampened the gunpowder.

Andrew Jackson, to his dying day, never believed that Richard Lawrence was a "lone assassin." It was Jackson's theory that Lawrence was a small cog in a vast plot to murder him. Behind it all, Jackson believed, was the Whig Party, which contained many of Jackson's political foes.

The president's enemies in the political arena had another theory. They claimed that Jackson and his supporters had staged the assassination attempt in an effort to win public sympathy.

Both theories were widely circulated. It seemed that few people of the day were willing to accept the fact that a crackpot could bring down a president, a great national hero. It was thus established early in the nation's history that a presidential assassin, successful or not, could easily trigger tales of vast conspiracies, with no supporting evidence at all.

2
Murder in Box 7

Friday, April 14, 1865, dawned cloudy and damp in Washington. The city was slow to come alive, for most people were tired and hungover from several days of celebrating.

The cause of their rejoicing was the news that had been received several days before, on April 9, that General Robert E. Lee had surrendered to General Ulysses S. Grant at Appomattox Court House in Virginia.

After four long years, the Civil War was drawing to an end. "I've never been so happy in my life," President Abraham Lincoln kept saying.

That morning, the president had breakfast with his family — his wife and their two sons, Tad, who had recently passed his twelfth birthday,

and Robert, twenty-one, who had recently returned from a tour of duty with General Grant.
Lincoln listened intently to Robert's opinions of
Grant and his impressions of the last days of the
war.

Mrs. Lincoln mentioned she had tickets for
Grover's Theatre that evening, where a huge victory celebration was to be staged. But she said
she would rather see Laura Keene, who was star-
ring in *Our American Cousin* at Ford's Theatre.

*The last photographic portrait of Abraham Lincoln, taken about
twelve weeks before his death. (Line at the top of the photograph is
the result of a crack in the glass negative.)*

The president said he would make the arrangements.

Mrs. Lincoln wanted to know whether General Grant and his wife would be going with them to the theatre. The president said he thought they would be.

After breakfast, the president went to his office in the White House. He signed a few documents and met with several visitors. Members of his cabinet began arriving for their regular Friday meeting.

At around ten-thirty at Ford's Theatre, a red-brick structure that had once been a Baptist church, a messenger arrived from the White House with the news that the President and Mrs. Lincoln and General and Mrs. Grant would be attending that evening's performance. Harry Ford, the theatre's manager, smiled when he read the message. He realized a presidential visit would assure a full house for the evening.

Ford began at once to make preparations for the presidential party. He removed a partition from between Boxes 7 and 8, creating a large seating area for the president and his guests. He furnished the space with two stuffed chairs, a few straight-backed chairs, and a rocking chair that he thought the president might find comfortable.

Ford draped the blue and gold flag of the United States Treasury Guards, an organization of federal employees that had been formed to defend the capital, across the outside of the boxes, just

A view of the stage at Ford's Theatre. The presidential box, decorated with flags and a framed picture of George Washington, is at the right.

below two American flags. He hung a framed picture of George Washington between the two boxes, facing the stage.

The president's meeting with his cabinet lasted until one-thirty in the afternoon. The main topic of discussion was Reconstruction, how the former Confederate states might be brought back into the Union. Afterward, the president left his office to have lunch with Mrs. Lincoln.

That afternoon, the president walked over to the War Department, the building just to the west of the White House (now the Old Executive Office Building). A bodyguard, William Crook, went with him.

There was no Secret Service protection for the president in those days. Instead the Washington metropolitan police force furnished men to the White House to protect the president. Two of these men were William Crook and John Parker. On that fateful April Friday in 1865, Crook had been assigned the tour of duty from eight o'clock in the morning to four in the afternoon. He was then to be replaced by Parker, the night man.

On the way over to the War Department, Lincoln noticed some drunken men making a scene. "Crook," the President said, "do you know I believe there are some men who want to take my life?" Lincoln then paused and added, "and I have no doubt they will do it."

Crook was surprised. He had never heard the president speak in such terms. "I hope you are mistaken, Mr. President," he said.

At the War Department, Lincoln asked Secretary of War Edwin Stanton whether Major Thomas T. Eckert, chief of the War Department's telegraph office, might go with him and Mrs. Lincoln to the theatre that night. Eckert was tall and strong and Lincoln thought highly of him as a bodyguard.

Stanton said he was sorry but Eckert had other duties that night. Stanton had a reason for telling the president that Eckert was unavailable. He didn't want Lincoln to go out in public yet. Washington was in great turmoil after the war and Stanton didn't think it was safe. So he denied Lincoln's request, hoping to persuade the president to cancel his plans for the evening.

When Lincoln left the War Department to return to the White House, he made it clear to Crook that he did not intend to change his plans. "It has been advertised that we will be there and I cannot disappoint the people," said Lincoln. "Otherwise, I would not go."

At four o'clock that afternoon, when it came time for Crook to be relieved, John Parker, his replacement, did not appear. An hour passed, then two. Still no Parker. Crook was angry but he tried not to show it.

Parker's lateness was no surprise to Crook. The man was often careless and thoughtless. Throughout his career as a police officer, he had been guilty of one wrong-headed move after another.

Thirty-four years old, married, the father of three children, Parker had served three months with the Union Army in 1861. The same year, he had been accepted as a police officer by the metropolitan police.

During his first year on the force, Parker had been suspended for using profane language. Later, he was charged with insulting a woman who had asked for police protection.

In April 1863, Parker was charged with being drunk and disorderly, but found not guilty. Two weeks later, he was charged with sleeping on a streetcar. He said he had boarded the streetcar to investigate the squawking of ducks. During the investigation, he had fallen asleep.

It seems incredible that John F. Parker could have been assigned to protect the life of President Lincoln.

It was after seven o'clock when Parker came strolling down the White House corridor to relieve Crook. He was more than three hours late.

"The president is going to the theatre tonight," Crook said, forcing back his anger. "You will go with him."

"Are you armed?" Crook asked. Parker said he was.

When the president appeared at the office door for a moment, Crook said, "Good night, Mr. President."

The president looked at him and said, "Goodbye, Crook."

On the way home, Crook kept thinking about the president's response. Always before, he had said, "*Good night*, Crook."

Later at the White House, the Lincolns were having problems putting their guest list together. It had been originally planned that General and Mrs. Grant would be going to the theatre with them, and it had even been announced in the newspapers. But Mrs. Grant could not stand the high strung Mrs. Lincoln, and the Grants backed out of the invitation. Early that evening, they left by train to visit their children in Burlington, New Jersey.

As substitutes for the Grants, the Lincolns invited a young engaged couple, Major Henry Reed Rathbone and his fiancée Clara Harris, the daughter of Ira Harris, a United States Senator from New York. Lincoln had recently appointed the twenty-eight-year-old Major Rathbone to be assistant adjutant of volunteers.

The Lincolns were late in getting started that evening. It was shortly after eight o'clock when their horse-drawn carriage pulled away from the White House. They stopped at Senator Harris's home to pick up Clara Harris and Major Rathbone. From there, the party headed directly to the theatre, a short drive.

It was almost eight-thirty when the Lincolns arrived, on a night that had become cold and drizzly. On both sides of Tenth Street, other carriages were parked. People stood at the windows of small houses and gathered in clusters on the sidewalk in front of the theatre, hoping to catch a glimpse of the president.

John Parker had gone to the theatre ahead of the presidential party, walking over from the White House. He went upstairs and gave Box 7 a quick inspection. Everything looked all right.

Parker was there to lead the presidential party

into the theatre and up the stairs to Boxes 7 and 8. The play had already begun. When the president, Mrs. Lincoln, and their guests entered, members of the audience stood and began to applaud. Then Laura Keene, the star of the play, saw the president, stopped the action onstage and began to applaud enthusiastically. Then the entire audience of more than 1,600 stood and applauded. The band struck up "Hail to the Chief." The audience watched as Clara Harris and Major Rathbone took their seats in Box 8, and then Mrs. Lincoln and the president entered Box 7. The president's figure was partly hidden by drapes.

When the band had finished and the audience had applauded again, the play resumed. The Lincolns and their guests settled down to watch. John Parker took up his post in the corridor outside the presidential box. It bothered him that he could not see the stage from his chair.

Our American Cousin told of an unpolished and clownish American backwoodsman who visits very proper cousins in their English country home. Mrs. Lincoln laughed heartily at every joke. The president leaned forward in his rocking chair, resting his chin on one hand. His thoughts often seemed elsewhere.

During the play, the president noticed that Major Rathbone had taken Clara Harris's hand in his. So he reached over to find Mrs. Lincoln's hand and held it at the side of his rocker. When he continued to hold it, Mrs. Lincoln leaned close to him and said, "What will Miss Harris think of my hand hanging onto you so?"

"Why," the president said, not turning from the play, "she will think nothing about it." He continued to hold his wife's hand.

At the end of Act 1, when the house lights were turned up, many in the audience stood and studied the figures in the presidential box. Most could not see Lincoln plainly, only a seated figure in shadows.

After the play resumed, John Parker became bored. He got up, walked downstairs, and out of the theatre. On the street outside he saw the president's carriage. In the seat atop the carriage, Parker spotted Francis Burns, the president's coachman.

"How would you like a little ale?" Parker said.

That sounded like a good idea to Burns. The two men headed for Taltavul's, a tavern next door to the theatre. Charles Forbes, Lincoln's valet, came out of the theatre to join them.

While at the bar, Parker and his cronies are almost certain to have rubbed elbows with twenty-six-year-old John Wilkes Booth, one of the country's most noted actors. He had been drinking through much of the day. Handsome, with dark hair and deep-set eyes, Booth was planning to assassinate Lincoln that very night. At the same time, other members of the small band of conspirators he had formed were planning to kill

Vice President Andrew Johnson and Secretary of State William Seward.

Booth approved of slavery and sympathized with the South during the Civil War. He believed that Lincoln was responsible for the war and the problems of the South. "Our country owed all her troubles to him," he wrote in his diary, "and God simply made me the instrument of his punishment."

Booth was born near Bel Air, Maryland, in

While John Wilkes Booth was a skilled actor, he lacked the talent of his brother, Edwin, and his father, Junius.

1838. His father, Junius Booth, was originally an English actor who gained great fame in the United States. His brother Edwin, five years older than John, is recognized as one of the greatest actors in the history of the American stage. John, not as skilled or as experienced as Edwin, achieved his greatest popularity in the South.

Only a few months before, Lincoln had seen John perform at Ford's Theatre. The president sat in the box he now occupied and watched Booth play the role of a villain. Whenever the fiery actor had anything hateful or threatening to say, he had stepped near to the presidential box and, shaking his finger toward Lincoln, had said the words directly to him. "He looks as if he meant that for you," a companion of the president said.

Booth had been planning to kidnap Lincoln for months, and had met regularly with the small band he had lured into the conspiracy. At one time, they planned to kidnap Lincoln and drag him in chains to Richmond, Virginia, and hold him there until Southern prisoners had been freed and Union armies had laid down their arms. Just three weeks earlier, Booth and his co-conspirators had surrounded and stopped the president's carriage. But inside they found someone else, not Lincoln. Booth changed the plot from kidnapping to murder after the main Confederate army surrendered on April 9, 1865.

Earlier that Friday, April 14, Booth had gone to Ford's Theatre to pick up his mail. He happened to overhear the manager say the president would attend the theatre that night. Booth could hardly believe his ears. After months of scheming, he had accomplished nothing. Now the president was to be practically delivered into his hands. It was an opportunity he could not let pass.

Booth spent the rest of the day plotting. The first thing he did was make arrangements to reserve a small bay mare which would be his means of escape.

Booth is also believed to have returned to Ford's Theatre that afternoon to bore a small hole in the door of Box 7, just behind the president's rocker. Through the hole, a person could view the people in the box.

A little hallway led to the box. Booth brought a pine board with him. By placing one end of the board against the closed hallway door and the other end against the wall, he could jam the door shut, and no one could open it from the outside. Alone in the hallway with the board in place, Booth could not be interfered with.

At around six-thirty that evening, Booth had supper. Afterward, he had a final meeting with his accomplices. Vice President Andrew Johnson and Secretary of State William Seward were to be killed at the same moment Booth himself was shooting the president.

At nine-thirty that evening, Booth rode the mare he had rented into the alley behind Ford's Theatre. He got a messenger boy to hold the mare's bridle and entered the theatre through the stage entrance.

At about this time, Lincoln leaned over to his wife and said he felt a chill. The president stood, put on his black coat, and then settled back into the rocker again.

Booth knew the play well and could mouth every line as the actors spoke them. He listened backstage for a few minutes before making his way through a passage under the stage to Tenth Street in front of the entrance to the theatre. He chatted with friends there for a while and then went into Taltavul's tavern for a drink.

The bar at Taltavul's was very busy. Booth spotted a group of friends and joined them. John Parker was there with Lincoln's coachman and valet. So was William Withers, Jr., the orchestra leader at Ford's Theatre. Booth called him over and ordered more drinks.

Someone at the bar lifted his glass to Booth and said to him, "You'll never be the actor your father was."

Booth replied with a smile. "When I leave the stage," he said, "I will be the most famous man in America."

The play was more than half over. Booth came out of Taltavul's and stood chatting with friends in front of the theatre. An admirer of Booth's came up to him and invited him to have a drink.

Booth shook his head. "Keene will be onstage in a minute," he said, "and I promised to take a look at her." It was shortly after ten o'clock.

Booth walked to the theatre's main entrance. Like other actors, he was not expected to pay. But John Buckingham, the ticket-taker, happened to put out his hand. Booth grinned and said, "You will not be needing a ticket from *me*."

Buckingham laughed, realizing his mistake. "Courtesy of the house," he said.

Booth stood at the back of the theatre for a few moments. Then he walked upstairs to the boxes. He was still in riding clothes, including high boots and spurs.

As Booth approached the door that opened into the hallway leading to Boxes 7 and 8, he looked about for John Parker. All he saw was Parker's empty chair.

Booth turned the knob, pushed open the door, and edged into the dark hallway. After closing the door, he jammed it shut with the pine board.

Now Booth, alone in the darkness, reached for his pistol, a brass-barreled, one-shot Derringer, only six inches long. A gleam of light came from the hole he had drilled in the door leading to Box 7. Booth put his eye to the hole. He could see the high-backed rocking chair and the back of the president's head above it.

A funny scene was unfolding and Booth could hear the actors. A Mrs. Montchessington, addressing Asa Trenchard, said, "I am aware, Mr. Trenchard, that you are not used to the manners of good society, and that alone will excuse the impertinence of which you have been guilty." With that, she stalked from the stage.

Now the stage was empty except for Asa Trenchard, who said, "Don't have the manners of good society, eh?" That was the line that Booth had been waiting for. The pistol in one hand, he turned the knob with the other, and slowly pushed the door open.

On the stage, Asa Trenchard continued, "Well I guess I know enough to turn you inside out, you sockdologizing old mantrap!" Booth knew that line would draw loud laughter, which would blot out the noise of the pistol.

Booth put the pistol behind the president's head and pulled the trigger. The box exploded in sound. After shooting Lincoln, Booth shouted *"Sic semper tyrannis!"* — thus be it ever to tyrants.

The handmade lead bullet, the size of a child's marble, flattened out as it pierced Lincoln's skull and dug into his brain. Lincoln slumped in his chair. The bewildered Mrs. Lincoln grasped the president about the neck and tried to keep him upright.

Booth threw down the empty pistol and pulled out a dagger. Major Rathbone lunged for Booth and grabbed his right arm. Booth slashed Rathbone in the left arm, the blade of his knife cutting to the bone.

As Rathbone reached for him a second time, Booth climbed over the railing and leaped the twelve feet to the stage. But as he dropped, the spur of his right foot caught in the Treasury Guards' flag that draped the railing. Booth landed off balance on his left foot, snapping the bone above the ankle.

Booth scrambled to his feet, faced the audience for a moment and said something like "The South is avenged." (His exact words are uncertain.)

Suddenly, a scream rang out. It was Mrs. Lincoln. "Help! Help! Help!" she shrieked.

In leaping from the box to the stage, Booth broke his leg, an injury that hindered his escape.

Someone yelled out, "He has shot the president!"

By this time, Booth had made his way to the alley in the back of the theatre and seized his horse from the young man in whose care he had placed it. He struggled onto the horse, then rode off into the dark. He followed a route that took him to Pennsylvania Avenue, then across the Navy Yard bridge and into southern Maryland.

The aisles at Ford's Theatre were now jammed with people. Some tried to force open the hallway door that Booth had barred shut. When he heard their pounding, Major Rathbone rushed to remove the pine board and open it.

Dr. Charles Leale, twenty-three years old, assistant surgeon of the United States Volunteers, was the first doctor to reach Lincoln's side. The president was being supported in his chair by Mrs. Lincoln. "Oh, Doctor," she cried, "do what you can for my husband. Is he dead? Will he recover?"

Dr. Leale said he would do what he could. He motioned to several men to take Mrs. Lincoln into the adjoining box. She sat on the sofa there. Clara Harris sat beside her, patting her hand.

After examining the paralyzed president and finding the gaping hole at the back of his head, Dr. Leale stood up and said, "His wound is mortal. It is impossible for him to recover."

Eager to get the president to the nearest bed, Dr. Leale ordered the president to be carried to

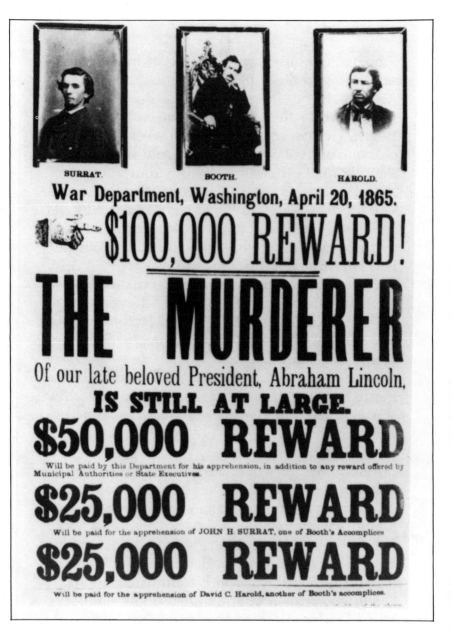

The federal government offered huge rewards for the capture of Booth and the other suspects.

a boarding house across the street from the theatre. Lincoln died there early the next morning, April 15.

Meanwhile, the hunt had begun for John Wilkes Booth. He met up in Maryland with David Herold, one of his accomplices. Herold had acted as a guide for Lewis Paine, who had attacked William Seward, Lincoln's secretary of state, with a knife, slashing his neck and right cheek. Seward recovered, however. George Atzerodt, the conspirator assigned to kill Vice President Johnson, had gotten drunk instead.

Were it not for his broken leg, Booth might have escaped. But the pain he suffered forced him to seek medical treatment. He and Herold located Dr. Samuel Mudd, a Maryland doctor, who put splints on Booth's leg.

In the days that followed, Booth lived like a hunted animal. On April 26, twelve days after the shooting, he and Herold were finally trapped in a tobacco shed on a farm outside Port Royal, Virginia. They were ordered out by Union soldiers, but only Herold would surrender.

When Booth could not be persuaded to give up, soldiers set fire to the barn. A figure could be seen hobbling about inside. A shot rang out and Booth fell. Later, a Union soldier, Sergeant Boston Corbett, said he had fired it. But another widely believed theory is that Booth committed suicide.

Soldiers rushed in and pulled Booth out of the burning barn. He died soon after. His last words were, "Tell Mother I die for my country."

Even before Booth's death, the government had named nine other persons who were involved in the assassination in one way or another. Except for one who escaped to Europe, all were tried before a military commission (and thus did not have the benefit of a trial by jury).

Many witnesses who should have been called were not. One was John Parker, who had left Lincoln unguarded. Parker was never made to pay for his neglect of duty.

Abraham Lincoln's funeral procession on Pennsylvania Avenue in Washington.

Four of the accused were sentenced to hang. On July 7, 1865, they went to their death. Three others were handed life sentences and one received a six-year term. Three of the four were later pardoned by President Andrew Johnson. The fourth had already died in prison.

Ford's Theatre and the "House Where Lincoln Died" have been preserved and are open to visitors today. The buildings and the furnishings they contain stand as monuments to one of the saddest and most momentous days in American history.

3
The Job Seeker

The American people had scarcely recovered from the horror of Abraham Lincoln's murder when, just sixteen years later, on July 2, 1881, James Garfield was gunned down by a man who wanted the president to give him a job as a diplomat. Garfield, the nation's twentieth president, did not die immediately. He lingered through the summer, and died on September 19, 1881.

There was no radio or TV in those days, but the American public kept up-to-date on Garfield's condition through daily newspapers and bulletins transmitted by telegraph. Said the New York *Tribune*: "By the everyday miracle of the telegraph and the printing press, the whole mass of people have been admitted to his bedside."

In the four months Garfield served as president, he spent much of his time feuding with Congress. Nevertheless, he was known to be friendly and easygoing.

Born in a shanty in Cuyahoga County, Ohio, in 1831, Garfield was the last log cabin president. His father died when he was two years old. As a boy, James worked as a canal bargeman, driving the horses and mules that pulled the boats on the canal towpath. Garfield also farmed and worked as a carpenter, using the money he earned to put himself through school and college.

James Garfield, the nation's twentieth president, was the second to be assassinated.

After he graduated from Williams College in Williamstown, Massachusetts, Garfield became a professor of Latin and Greek at Hiram Institute in Portage, Ohio. He was elected to the Ohio state senate in 1859.

When the Civil War loomed and President Lincoln issued a call for volunteers, Garfield signed up. He became a colonel of the 42nd Ohio Infantry. He performed with such brilliance that within a year he was a brigadier general. He was made a major general for his heroism at the battle of Chickamauga.

While still in the army, Garfield was elected to the House of Representatives. He served in the House for the next eighteen years. In 1880, he was elected to the U.S. Senate from Ohio.

When the Republicans met in Chicago in 1880 to choose a presidential candidate, the two favorites were James C. Blaine and Ulysses S. Grant, who had already served two presidential terms. The delegates were unable to choose between the two men. They voted thirty-five times without coming to a decision. Finally, on the thirty-sixth ballot, the delegates compromised on Garfield.

In the election that fall, Garfield managed to defeat his Democratic rival, Winfield Scott Hancock, by the slim margin of only 7,023 votes. Almost nine million votes were cast.

Within only a short time after being inaugurated, Garfield began to be stalked by his eventual assassin. The man who wanted to shoot the president was Charles Guiteau (pronounced ghi-TOE). Thirty-nine years old, ten years younger than the president, Guiteau had been a lawyer, evangelist, and author, but always unsuccessfully. He had also established himself as a cheat and a swindler.

Like the president, Guiteau wore a mustache and a full beard, which was the custom of the day. Smallish, he stood only five-foot-five and weighed about 125 pounds. He had a fidgety manner.

Charles Guiteau,
Garfield's assassin.

After Garfield had been nominated, Guiteau went to New York to offer his services to the Republicans in their efforts to get him elected. Guiteau asked for assignments as a paid speaker, but was quickly turned down.

Guiteau had composed a speech titled, "Garfield Against Hancock." It declared that Garfield's election would usher in a period of peace and prosperity. Guiteau paid to have the speech printed and handed out copies to Republican leaders. He asked them how they liked it and they said they did. Not realizing they were simply being polite, Guiteau was thrilled.

He spent much of the campaign hanging around Republican headquarters in New York, introducing himself to Republican leaders. He often discussed what job he might be awarded after Garfield had been elected. But the campaign workers regarded Guiteau as a pest. They wished he'd go away.

What Guiteau wanted was a diplomatic post in Europe. One day he came upon General Grant in the lobby of the Fifth Avenue Hotel in New York and asked him to sign a letter recommending Charles Guiteau to be named ambassador to Austria. Grant could hardly believe what he was hearing. He abruptly rejected the request.

Guiteau did not give up. Several weeks before the election, he sent a copy of his speech to Garfield himself at his home in Mentor, Ohio. In a letter to Garfield, he mentioned that he would like to become the Austrian ambassador. Garfield did not reply to the letter or acknowledge receiving the speech.

After Garfield won the election, Guiteau went to Washington, still seeking an ambassador's post in Austria or the "Paris consulship." Not long after his arrival, Guiteau managed, along with a mob of other jobseekers, to get to see the president in his White House office.

"As soon as General Garfield was at his leisure," Guiteau was later to say, "I stepped up to him and gave him my speech. I told him that I was an applicant for the Paris consulship, and he looked at it, and I left him reading the speech and retired."

Within a few days, a White House secretary told Guiteau his request had been turned over to the State Department. He then began to make regular visits there, leaving notes for James G. Blaine, who served as secretary of state in the Garfield administration.

Guiteau also sought to have members of Congress sign a petition that read, "We recommend Charles J. Guiteau for the Paris consulship." But none ever signed it.

One day Guiteau happened to meet Secretary Blaine in a corridor of the State Department. Immediately he asked Blaine about the consul's post in Paris. Blaine, who had managed to avoid Guiteau in his previous visits, glared at him. "Never speak to me about the Paris consulship as long as you live," he shouted.

Guiteau held his ground. "I'm going to see the president about this," he said.

But when Guiteau turned up at the White House gate, he was refused entry. The guards had been instructed to bar him.

Meanwhile, Garfield was having problems much more serious than those involving Charles Guiteau. A dispute over jobs had flared up between the president and a faction of the Republican Party known as the Stalwarts. There was no Civil Service in those days to screen and hire applicants for government employment. The final responsibility for all hiring rested with the president. The Stalwarts wanted to keep this policy unchanged.

Guiteau, who thought of himself as a Stalwart, was deeply distressed by the conflict. This added to his frustration.

He now began to toy with the idea of assassinating the president. The removal of Garfield would solve all of his problems, Guiteau believed. Upon his death, Garfield would be succeeded by Vice President Chester A. Arthur, who Guiteau knew to be a leader of the Stalwarts.

Early in June, Guiteau visited a gun shop not far from the White House and arranged to buy a .44 caliber British pistol with a white bone handle. (The term caliber refers to the inside diameter of a gun's barrel. In the United States, caliber is expressed in hundredths of an inch — .22, .30, .32, .38, .44, etc.) The shop owner said it "would kill a horse."

Guiteau did not have the money to pay for the pistol at the time. But after borrowing fifteen dollars from his cousin, he returned to the shop and completed the purchase. Since Guiteau had little or no experience with guns, the shopkeeper instructed him how to load and fire the weapon. He told Guiteau there was a wooded area along the Potomac River where he could try out the gun without endangering anyone. The next day, Guiteau practiced firing using tree trunks as targets.

Guiteau at first thought he might simply shoot the president in the White House but decided that would be too risky. Instead, he passed the time sitting on a bench in Lafayette Park, directly across Pennsylvania Avenue from the White House, waiting for the president to come out. Sometimes he would ask a White House guard when he could expect to see the president.

One Sunday in June, the president, riding in his horse-drawn carriage, attended church on Vermont Avenue. Guiteau followed and stood in the back of the church during services. In his pocket, Guiteau carried the loaded pistol. He considered shooting the president during the services but abandoned the plan because he thought he might injure other worshippers.

Not long after, Guiteau read in a local newspaper that the president was planning a trip to Long Branch, New Jersey, with Mrs. Garfield, who had been ill. The presidential party would be leaving on Saturday, June 18, from the Baltimore & Potomac Railroad Station, the newspaper said. The station, which has since been demolished, was located at Sixth Street and Constitution Avenue in Washington, now the site of the National Gallery of Art. The location is less than a mile southeast of Ford's Theatre, where Abraham Lincoln was shot.

Guiteau went to the station and waited for the Garfields to arrive. But when he saw the couple at close range, he lost his courage. "Mrs. Garfield looked so thin, and she clung so tenderly to the president's arm," Guiteau was to say later, "that I did not have the heart to fire on him."

But Guiteau had not changed his mind about shooting the president. He returned to the bench at Lafayette Park to wait for another opportunity.

He did not have to wait very long. At around seven o'clock on the evening of July 1, Guiteau watched intently as the president left the White House on foot, crossed Pennsylvania Avenue, and walked toward Madison Place, a short street that borders Lafayette Park to the east. His heart pounding, Guiteau followed the president. He watched as Garfield entered the home of James G. Blaine, the secretary of state. By coincidence, it was the very same house that had once been occupied by William Seward, Lincoln's secretary of state, and where Lewis Paine had tried to stab him to death sixteen years before.

As the daylight faded, Guiteau waited and watched. If Garfield emerged alone, he intended to shoot him.

But when Garfield came out, he was not alone; Blaine was with him. The two men walked back to the White House, ". . . as hilarious as two schoolgirls."

Guiteau did not make an attempt on Garfield's life that night because he "felt tired and wearied." Besides, he knew from an article in a newspaper that the president was leaving the next day by train from the Baltimore & Potomac station on a vacation trip.

The next morning, Guiteau was up before daybreak. He took a walk and read a newspaper. After having breakfast in the hotel where he was staying, Guiteau wrote some letters that explained why he intended to kill the president. "The president's death was a sad necessity," one of the letters said, "but it will unite the Republican Party and save the Republic."

Guiteau put the letter in a small package which he took to the station. He was wearing a black coat, white shirt, black vest, black trousers, and a wide-brimmed black hat that he pulled down to shield his eyes. In his right hip pocket, he carried the revolver. When he arrived at the station, he left the package with the operator of a newsstand. He hoped it would later be turned over to the police — and it was. Besides the letters, the package contained a brief autobiography and a note that willed his papers and pistol to the State Department.

After he had disposed of the package, Guiteau went into the men's room where he examined the pistol to be sure it was in good working condition. Then he went into the station to wait for the president.

Garfield was also up early that morning. After four months of work in the White House, he was looking forward to his vacation. Two weeks long, it was to include some boating on the Hudson River. Garfield also planned to attend the twenty-fifth reunion of his graduating class at Williams College.

Around nine o'clock, the president and James G. Blaine set off for the station in a horse-drawn carriage. The carriage arrived at the station at about nine-twenty, ten minutes before the president's train was scheduled to depart.

When Garfield and Blaine entered the station, Guiteau was already there. Walking side by side, the two men started crossing through the ladies' waiting room on the way to the train. Guiteau drew the pistol from his hip pocket. When Garfield and Blaine were about three quarters of the way across the room, Guiteau strode to within a few feet of the president and shot him in the back.

Guiteau fired twice, hitting President Garfield in the shoulder and back.

"My God, what is this!" Garfield cried. He flung up his arms and began to stagger. Blaine gasped in horror.

Guiteau fired again. The bullet passed through Garfield's right sleeve.

As the president crumpled to the floor, Guiteau turned and ran. But a policeman named Patrick Kearney grabbed him.

Guiteau was calm. "It's all right. Keep quiet my friend," he said. "I wish to go to jail."

Guiteau had made preparations for imprisonment. At police headquarters, he gave officers a letter to General William T. Sherman, the commander of the army, requesting that troops take over the jail to prevent violence. "I am a Stalwart," Guiteau proclaimed, "and Arthur is president."

Meanwhile, Garfield was taken to an office on the second floor of the station, where Blaine and others tried to make him comfortable. Doctors determined the bullet had entered the president's back just above the third rib. After an hour or so, the president was taken to the White House in a horse-drawn police ambulance.

The president's Cabinet and administration officials were summoned. Robert T. Lincoln, the son of Abraham Lincoln, who served as Garfield's secretary of war, was especially disturbed by the shooting. He could not help but recall the terrible night sixteen years before when his father had been the victim of an assassin's bullet. "My God, how many hours of sorrow have I passed in this town!" he said.

Closer examination of the president revealed that Guiteau's bullet had fractured two of Garfield's ribs and one of the bones in his spinal column, and cut an important artery. The bullet had stopped behind the pancreas, a soft gland near the stomach that produces fluid important to digestion.

One of Garfield's doctors was Joseph K. Barnes,

surgeon general of the army, who had come to the aid of Lincoln after he had been shot. But neither Barnes nor any of the other doctors who attended Garfield were able to determine exactly how serious the president's wounds were, largely because they had no x-ray equipment. More than a decade was to pass before the x-ray was discovered.

Alexander Graham Bell, the inventor of the telephone, sought to assist the doctors with a device that he believed could pinpoint the location of the bullet in Garfield's stomach. The equipment worked on the same principle as a metal detector of the present day, giving off a hum in the presence of certain metals. Bell's device signaled the bullet was lodged about where doctors had indicated, but it could not determine how deeply it had gone. Because of the president's weakened condition, no attempt was made to remove the bullet.

Through the steamy Washington summer, the president battled for his life. The first reports were encouraging, but toward the end of July his temperature shot up to 104 degrees. Apparently, blood poisoning had set in. Had modern antibiotics been available, the infection could have been brought under control.

Early in August, the president rallied for a time. He began ordering his own meals, which he ate heartily. On August 10, he managed to sign an official paper, the first since the shooting.

But in mid-August, there was a change for the worse, and Garfield's strength declined sharply. He asked his doctors whether he could be moved to Elberon on the New Jersey shore, where the sea air might help him. The doctors agreed the change might be helpful.

Early in September, the president's bed was carried from the White House and placed in a horse-drawn express wagon, taken to the train station, and placed aboard a railroad car. Especially prepared for comfort, the train carried the president north to Elberon. Along the way, all the tracks were cleared and the bells and whistles silenced so Garfield would not be disturbed. Temporary tracks had been laid to the house where he was to stay.

The trip seemed to do the president no harm. But by mid-September, the fever would not leave him and he grew steadily weaker. The infection was ravaging his entire body.

For several days, his life hung in balance. The ordeal ended with his death on September 19, 1881.

Vice President Chester Alan Arthur was at his father's townhouse in New York City when he was told of the president's death. Early the next morning, he took the oath of office in the front parlor of the house.

On September 21, Garfield's body was taken to Washington to lie in state in the rotunda of the Capitol. He was buried at the Lake View Ceme-

THE LAST BULLETIN.

ELBERON, N. J.,
SEPT. 19, 11.30 P. M.

The President died at 10.35. After the bulletin was issued at half-past five this evening the President continued in much the same condition as during the afternoon, the pulse varying from 102 to 106, with rather increased force and volume. After taking nourishment he fell into a quiet sleep about thirty-five minutes before his death, and while asleep his pulse rose to 120, and was somewhat more feeble. At ten minutes after ten o'clock he awoke, complaining of severe pain over the region of the heart, and almost immediately became unconcious, and ceased to breathe at 10:35.

D. W. BLISS.
F. H. HAMILTON.
D. H. AGNEW.

Garfield's doctors issued this bulletin upon his death.

tery in Cleveland, Ohio. Friends of the Garfields helped to raise a large fund to help support Mrs. Garfield and the children.

During Arthur's administration, Congress passed legislation that created the Civil Service Commission and a system of hiring jobseekers on the basis of tests and interviews.

Two months after Garfield's death, Guiteau's trial began. For the ten and a half weeks it lasted, Guiteau often behaved like a lunatic. He interrupted the proceedings whenever he felt like it with comments and speeches. He called the prosecutor "an old hog" and "a fraud." He referred to witnesses as "low, dirty liars," and his own lawyer as a "jackass."

Day after day, the courtroom was packed with spectators eager to watch Guiteau perform. They cheered and hissed his outbursts. It was a circus.

Early in the trial, Guiteau argued that the doctors who had treated Garfield were responsible for his death. He pointed out that in the weeks following the shooting, the doctors had announced that the president would recover. In other words, the attempt at assassination had failed. Said Guiteau: "The doctors who mistreated him ought to bear the odium of his death, not his assailant."

Guiteau's lawyers tried to prove he was insane. But the government argued that Guiteau was no madman, only a disappointed jobseeker. When his request for a diplomatic post had been rejected, Guiteau had sought revenge. He was also motivated by a craving for publicity, said the government lawyers.

It took the jury only an hour and five minutes to reach a verdict. They found Guiteau to be sane — and guilty. He was sentenced to death by hanging.

On June 30, 1882, the date of Guiteau's execution, several thousand people gathered outside the jailhouse in Washington. More than 250 persons were admitted to watch the hanging.

Wardens' Office D. C. Jail.
Washington, D. C.

Mr.

You are respectfully invited to witness the execution of Charles J. Guiteau, at this jail Friday June 30th 1882; between the hours of 12 M., and 2 o'clock P. M.

John S. Crocker

Warden.

Guiteau's execution was a public event, with tickets issued to those who wished to witness it.

On the scaffold, Guiteau recited a poem he had written. In part, it said:

I am going to the Lordy, I am so glad . . .
I saved my party and my land; glory,
    hallelujah.
But they have murdered me for it, and that is
    the reason
I am going to the Lordy . . .

Guiteau was still talking as the hangman placed the black hood over his head and sprung the trap. "Glory, glory, glory," were his last words.

4
Attack by an Anarchist

Buffalo, New York, was an exciting place to be in the summer of 1901. The Pan-American Exposition was being held in the city, and many thousands of people visited the fair grounds each day.

They listened to John Philip Sousa's rousing band concerts and in the evening gazed at the Tower of Light, more than 400 feet high and studded with 35,000 light bulbs. Although Thomas Edison had demonstrated the first practical incandescent lamp some twenty-two years before, electrical illumination was still a novelty in the United States.

June 13 was named President's Day at the Exposition, and President William McKinley, the

25th president, whose policies had helped to make the United States a world power, was to visit. But Mrs. McKinley became seriously ill, so the president cancelled the trip.

Early in August, a new date was announced — September 5. On September 4, the McKinleys arrived in Buffalo from their home in Canton, Ohio, aboard a special train of the Lake Shore & Michigan Southern Railway. The next afternoon, the president, wearing a tall silk hat and black frock coat, delivered a speech at the fair grounds. More than fifty-thousand people cheered and applauded.

The day before his assassination, President McKinley addressed a huge crowd at the Pan American Exposition in Buffalo.

Leon Czolgosz (pronounced CHOL-gosh), a twenty-eight-year-old self-proclaimed anarchist, was standing among the cheering throng. He planned to shoot and kill the president. He fully understood what he was doing and was prepared to sacrifice his life. But the press of the crowd that afternoon made it impossible for Czolgosz to get close enough to the speaker's platform to carry out his mission.

Czolgosz knew that on the next day, September 6, the president planned to greet the public at a reception at the Temple of Music on the fair grounds. The Buffalo newspapers said that the president would exchange handshakes with his fellow citizens. Leon Czolgosz planned to be there.

Although in photographs President McKinley usually appears to be unsmiling and pompous, he was actually a gentle, dignified man, known for his kindness and compassion. He was deeply devoted to his wife, Ida, an invalid.

Born on January 29, 1843, in Niles, Ohio, McKinley was the seventh of nine children. A good student, he attended Allegheny College in Meadville, Pennsylvania.

When the Civil War erupted in 1861, McKinley was the first man in his hometown to volunteer. By the end of the war, he had risen from the enlisted ranks to become a brevet major.

After the war, McKinley became a lawyer and developed an interest in politics. Elected to the

U.S. House of Representatives from Ohio in 1876, he served almost continuously until 1890. The next year he was elected governor of Ohio. He was reelected in 1893.

As the Republican candidate for president in 1896, McKinley won a landslide victory over the great orator, William Jennings Bryan. America enjoyed a period of booming growth during McKinley's first term.

The president was also successful in foreign affairs. He led the country through the Spanish-American War, the most one-sided war the nation fought up until the Persian Gulf War in 1991. American soldiers and sailors defeated Spain, and as a result, the United States acquired Guam, the Philippines, and Puerto Rico. In the same time period Hawaii and American Samoa were acquired as colonies.

There was none of the sectional hatred that had helped to bring about the assassination of President Lincoln. Nor was the period marred by any of the interparty squabbling that had helped play a part in President Garfield's murder.

When McKinley ran for re-election in 1900, he won a sweeping victory, again defeating William Jennings Bryan. McKinley's vice president was Theodore Roosevelt, who had been acclaimed as a hero during the Spanish-American War and been elected governor of New York.

Leon Czolgosz did not have any particular hatred for President McKinley or his policies.

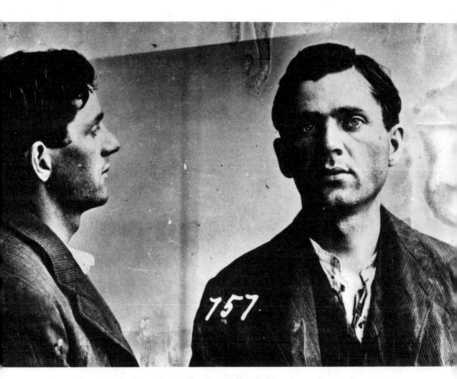
Leon Frank Czolgosz, McKinley's assassin.

Nevertheless, he felt it was his "duty" to shoot him.

"I thought it would be a good thing for the country to kill the president," Czolgosz said. "McKinley was going around the country shouting prosperity, when there was no prosperity for the working man."

Czolgosz thought of himself as an anarchist. Anarchists believe that the best government is no government, that all forms of government should be abolished in order to achieve full social and political liberty. Because they seek to overthrow the government, anarchists, though not great in number, were feared by many Americans of the 1890s in somewhat the same way communists were feared in the 1950s and 1960s.

Leon F. Czolgosz was born near Detroit in 1873, the fourth of eight children. His parents had recently immigrated from Poland, and both were hard working. His mother died not long after the birth of their last child.

When Leon was seven, the Czolgoszes moved to northern Michigan. There they lived in communities that were made up largely of Polish immigrants like themslves. Leon was brought up speaking both Polish and English.

Leon's schooling lasted for only five and a half years. During that time, he attended a public school, a Catholic parochial school, and night school. A quiet and willful boy who often kept to himself, Leon enjoyed books and reading more than anything else. He came to be looked upon as the best educated member of his family.

In 1889, when Leon turned sixteen, the family moved to Natrona, a Polish community near Pittsburgh. Leon went to work in a bottle factory. His job was to carry red-hot bottles on a pronged, shovel-like implement from the ovens to the place where they were cooled. His starting pay was 75 cents a day.

After two years in Natrona, the family moved

to Cleveland, and Leon got a job in a wire factory. He was a steady and reliable worker. He earned ten dollars a week. After several years, Leon managed to save four hundred dollars from his earnings, money which he contributetd toward the purchase of a family farm near Warrensville, Ohio, not far from Cleveland.

In 1893, the wire mill workers went on strike for higher pay. Czolgosz played an active role in the work stoppage, often addressing strikers' meetings. When the strike was settled, Leon, fearing the new boss might harbor a grudge against him, used the name "Fred G. Nieman."

The strike at the wire factory was a political awakening for Czolgosz. Within a year, he joined a Polish political discussion group in Cleveland. Anarchism was one of the topics often discussed. "I came to the opinion that our form of voting was not right," Czolgosz later said. "I discussed it and began to talk it over with the people that belonged to the circle." Czolgosz was also to admit the group discussed the presidents and decided "that they were no good."

At twenty-one years old, Czolgosz was five-feet, seven and a half inches tall, and weighed about 135 pounds. He had slightly stooped shoulders, a round, boyish-looking face, blue eyes, and wavy, light brown hair that he combed straight back. On his left cheek, he had a small scar, the result of an accident in the wire factory.

He was a quiet and distant young man, something of a loner. At meetings of discussion groups to which he belonged, he seldom spoke his opinions, but instead listened intently to what others had to say. At a saloon his father owned and operated, where Leon sometimes drank a glass of beer or an occasional whisky, he merely watched others play cards and other games. He preferred being a spectator and thus was thought by many to be shy and faint-hearted.

In 1898, when he was twenty-five, Czolgosz became ill. No one is sure of the nature of the illness, but it triggered a distinct change in his personality. Dr. Walter Channing, who, at the time, served as a professor of Mental Diseases at Tufts Medical College in Boston, undertook a study of Czolgosz, and noted that the illness changed him "from an industrious and apparently fairly normal young man into a sickly, unhealthy, and abnormal one."

Czolgosz quit his job at the wire factory in the summer of 1898, explaining that he was not well. He never again would have a regular job. He went to live on the family farm in Warrensville, where he spent his days sulking despondently and reading.

Several years before, his father had remarried, and Leon and his stepmother did not get along very well. The two sometimes quarreled heatedly. Czolgosz stopped having his meals with the family, preferring to stay in his room and prepare his meals there.

In the summer of 1900, an event occurred that caught Czolgosz's interest. On July 29 that year, King Umberto I of Italy was distributing prizes to athletes at the town of Monza, when a man stepped up to his carriage and pumped four bullets into his body, killing him. The assassin was a mill worker from Paterson, New Jersey, named Gaetano Bresci. An anarchist, Bresci had planned the murder for months. He eventually took a ship to Italy and carried out the plot.

No one knows if the killing of the Italian monarch gave Czolgosz the idea of assassinating President McKinley. It is known, however, that Czolgosz clipped the story of King Umberto's assassination from a local newspaper and read it over and over. He carried the article in his wallet and even took it to bed with him.

The following year, 1901, Czolgosz sought to strengthen his ties to American anarchists. He went to Cleveland to hear a lecture delivered by Russian-born Emma Goldman, a noted anarchist of the time. But Goldman's talk was probably a disappointment to Czolgosz. Although she raised her voice against the government, saying anarchism was the only true form of freedom, she did not favor violence and bomb-throwing.

That summer, Czolgosz visited anarchist leaders in Cleveland and Chicago. He tried to join anarchist clubs, but his strange ways and talk of violence disturbed the leaders. While Czolgosz began to think of himself as one of the anarchists, the truth was that they wanted nothing to do with him.

Later that summer, Czolgosz drifted to West Seneca, New York, a small town just outside Buffalo. There he rented a room over a saloon on Broadway.

Czolgosz visited the Pan-American Exposition frequently that summer. He was among the huge crowd that listened to the president and watched the military review held in his honor on September 5. Czolgosz didn't like what he saw. "I thought it wasn't right for any one man to get so much ceremony," he was to say later. "I saw a great many people there saluting him, bowing to him, and paying homage to him . . ."

Several days before, Czolgosz had made up his mind to murder the president. He had purchased a .32 caliber Iver Johnson revolver with an owl's head stamped on each side of the handle from a shop on Main Street, paying four dollars and fifty cents for it.

When Czolgosz read that the president was to hold a public reception at the Temple of Music, he realized it would offer a perfect opportunity for him to carry out his plan. The day of the reception, he arrived at the Temple of Music a full hour before the president was due.

Some members of McKinley's staff didn't like the idea of the president meeting the public. It was simply too risky. In everyone's mind there were memories of the shooting of King Umberto the previous summer. In addition, there had been rumors of an anarchist plot against the president. But when George Cortelyou, the president's secretary, sought to cancel the reception, McKinley wouldn't hear of it. "Why should I?" he said. "No one would wish to hurt me."

Many hundreds of people visited the fair grounds with the hope of shaking the president's hand. The Temple of Music was teeming with police in uniform, detectives, Secret Service agents, and even soldiers, all there to guard the president. Many were stationed only a few feet from him.

The president stood at the front of the Temple, with George Cortelyou on one side and John G. Milburn, the president of the Exposition, on the other. The president was wearing a black frock coat, a white shirt and white vest, a black tie, and dark trousers. It was an extremely hot day, and inside the Temple the temperature soared.

The people entered the Temple in orderly fashion, thanks to the many policemen and soldiers who kept everything peaceful. For the first forty or fifty feet, the people moved in pairs, but as they got close to the president, they fell into single file.

The line was so long that the president ordered it speeded up so he would be able to greet everyone who was waiting. Soon no one was really able to pause in front of the president; people simply grasped his fingers for a split second before moving on.

Czolgosz was near the front. As he edged his way toward the president, he drifted out of line. A soldier ordered him back in place. He obeyed immediately.

When it was almost his turn to shake the president's hand, Czolgosz reached into his hip pocket and took out the revolver. He quickly wrapped his right hand, the one holding the revolver, in a large handkerchief, then held the hand close to his body. Nobody thought anything was wrong. Sam Ireland, a Secret Service agent standing close to the president, noticed Czolgosz's bandaged right hand and thought he had burned himself.

Now Czolgosz was almost in front of the president. He put out his left hand and McKinley reached for it. At the same instant, Czolgosz thrust his right hand forward and fired two shots in rapid succession through the handkerchief.

The president slumped into the arms of the men who had been guarding him. Czolgosz stood in front of him, seemingly frozen, and mumbled something. Then suddenly he was attacked from all sides by Secret Service agents, police, and soldiers. They knocked him to the floor and began to pound him with their fists and butts of their guns. One of the soldiers seemed intent on stabbing him with his bayonet. The president called out, "Be easy with him, boys."

His right hand bandaged to conceal the gun, Czolgosz fired point blank at President McKinley.

After the shooting, this electric-powered ambulance hurried President McKinley to a nearby hospital.

An electric-powered ambulance took the president to an emergency hospital on the grounds of the Exposition. One bullet had struck the president in the breastbone. The other did far more damage, ripping into his belly and puncturing both walls of the stomach before coming to rest, doctors believed, in the muscles of his back.

That night, doctors operated on McKinley. They probed for the bullet that had entered his stomach but could not find it. After they had closed the president's wound, he was taken to the home of John G. Milburn, a lawyer who was serving as the Exposition president, where the McKinleys had been staying.

For several days, doctors were optimistic about McKinley's chances for recovery. But then he suddenly began to grow weaker. On September 13, as his condition continued to worsen, the president and his family realized he was dying. Around two o'clock on the morning of September 14, McKinley said his last words: "Good-bye, all. Good-bye. It is God's way. His will be done." Then he sank into a coma and died.

Later, the cause of death was announced as blood poisoning brought on by gangrene of the pancreas. But more recently it has been said that McKinley's death was caused, at least in part, by bungled surgery, by doctors who were hampered by not having the right surgical instruments and poor lighting in the operating room.

At the time of McKinley's death, Vice President Theodore Roosevelt was enjoying a mountain-climbing vacation in Vermont. A special train carried him to Buffalo. He took the oath of office there several hours after the president's death.

"Are you an anarchist?" the police asked Czolgosz after the shooting. "Yes," he answered.

He added that he bore no grudge against McKinley but that he did not believe in govern-

The headline from The Illustrated Buffalo Express *in Buffalo, New York, on September 15, 1901.*

ment of any kind — or in religion or marriage. "I killed McKinley because I done my duty," he wrote.

The law moved speedily to bring Czolgosz to trial. It got underway on September 23, just four days after McKinley's funeral in Canton, Ohio.

Two Buffalo lawyers were assigned to represent Czolgosz. They had a heavy burden. First, Czolgosz did not even talk with his defense team. Second, the two men had to cope with the fact that five doctors had agreed that Czolgosz was sane.

The trial lasted less than nine hours, including the time it took to select a jury. And it took only 34 minutes for the jury to reach a decision. Czolgosz was found guilty and sentenced to death.

On October 29, 1901, he was strapped into the electric chair at Auburn State Prison in New York and executed. Scarcely seven weeks had passed since he had fired the bullets that proved fatal to McKinley.

According to witnesses, Czolgosz was "calm . . . and self-possessed" in the minutes before the execution. "His face bore an expression of defiant determination."

Czolgosz said, "I killed the president because he was the enemy of the good people — the good working people. I am not sorry for my crime."

5
Saved by a Speech

Theodore Roosevelt was the youngest man to become president. He was 42 years and 322 days old when he took the oath of office in Buffalo, New York, in 1901, following the assassination of William McKinley. (John F. Kennedy was the youngest man *elected* to office. He was 43 years and 236 days old when he took the presidential oath in 1961.)

The twenty-sixth president was colorful and dynamic, a man of enormous energy. He enjoyed swimming, hunting, hiking, boxing, and horseback riding. During his two terms as president, Roosevelt wrote more than 150,000 letters. During his lifetime, he wrote thirty books. They covered a wide range of interests, everything from

70

Teddy Roosevelt was colorful and dynamic, a man of tremendous energy.

The Life of Oliver Cromwell to *Through the Brazilian Wilderness.*

Born in New York City in 1858, Roosevelt was thin, weak, and nervous as a child. His father built him a gym on the third floor of the family townhouse on 20th Street in New York. There he did chin-ups on an iron bar and pounded away at a heavy punching bag. As a college student at Harvard, he entered boxing tournaments (as a lightweight).

Roosevelt later was a rancher and New York's Police Commissioner. During the Spanish-American War in 1898, Roosevelt became a national hero as commander of the fearless Rough Riders. He led a famous cavalry charge against the Spanish in Cuba and won tremendous popularity. To most Americans, he was "Teddy" or "T.R."

During his two terms as president, Roosevelt became known as the "trust buster" because he tried to limit the power of big corporations. He supported laws that protected Americans from harmful foods and drugs and conserved the country's natural resources.

"Speak softly and carry a big stick" was the phrase used to describe Roosevelt's foreign policy. He strengthened the Navy and began construction of the Panama Canal. He got Russian and Japanese delegates to meet at Portsmouth, New Hampshire, and agree on peace, ending the war between those two nations. For this, he became the first president to win the Nobel Peace Prize.

After he retired from the presidency in 1909, Roosevelt hunted for big game in Africa and made a speaking tour of the West. He remained extremely popular and was frequently asked to run for a third term as president. Roosevelt normally rejected these suggestions, but in 1912 he eventually gave in to the pleas.

No American president had ever run for a third term before, although at the time there was no

Constitutional amendment prohibiting it. George Washington had declined a third term. So had Thomas Jefferson and Andrew Jackson. There was a tradition of only two terms.

Roosevelt himself had once told his Republican supporters that "under no circumstances" would he run a third time. But in 1912, he said that his earlier statement had meant not running for a third *consecutive* term.

William Howard Taft was president at the time Roosevelt started campaigning. Taft controlled the Republican Party and wanted the nomination for himself. So Roosevelt and his supporters formed a third party, the Progressive Party, nick-named the Bull Moose Party. The name came from Roosevelt's reply when a reporter once asked him how he felt. He replied with his usual enthusiasm, saying, "I feel as strong as a bull moose."

One person who violently opposed Roosevelt's plan to seek a third term was thirty-six-year-old John N. Schrank, a short and round-faced man with blue-gray eyes. "Let every third-termer be regarded as a traitor to the American cause . . ." Schrank wrote. He believed it was the "right and duty of every citizen to forcibly remove a third termer." Schrank felt so strongly about the issue he began to stalk Roosevelt along the campaign trail. He bought a gun and made plans to use it.

The fact that Roosevelt was seeking a third

John Schrank followed Roosevelt for more than a thousand miles before he made his attempt to assassinate him in Milwaukee.

term was only one of the reasons that Schrank wanted to do away with him. The other was bizarre. Schrank believed that Roosevelt was responsible for President McKinley's murder.

Schrank got this idea from a dream. In the early morning hours of September 15, 1901, almost twenty-four hours after McKinley had died, Schrank dreamed he was in a room in which there was a coffin surrounded by flowers. There was a person in the coffin and it was McKinley. Suddenly, McKinley sat straight up and pointed toward a corner of the room. There Schrank saw a man dressed as a monk, whom he recognized as Theodore Roosevelt.

"This is my murderer," McKinley declared from the coffin. "Avenge my death."

Schrank knew, of course, that it was Leon Czolgosz who had assassinated President McKinley. Nevertheless, the dream made a deep impression on him, and he thought of it frequently in the years that followed. It did not, however, make a great deal of sense to him until Roosevelt was nominated for a third term by the Progressive Party in August 1912. Schrank then became obsessed with the dream.

John Schrank was born in 1876 in a small town not far from Munich, in the German state of Bavaria. When he was a small child, his father, a brewery worker, died and his mother remarried and moved to another town. But instead of keeping John, she left him with Dominick and Anna Flammang, John's uncle and aunt.

When John was a young teenager, the Flammangs emigrated to the United States and settled in New York City. There Mr. Flammang bought a saloon in a German neighborhood on East Tenth Street. The family moved into an apartment on the floor above it.

Young John learned to speak English and before long became a naturalized American citizen. When he was fifteen, he began to help out his uncle by tending bar. He also delivered pails of beer to patrons who lived in nearby apartments.

From an early age, John was interested in history and politics. He always voted in local and national elections. He filled his spare time by reading books and newspapers. He also read the Bible, the Constitution, and the Declaration of Independence. His heroes included George Washington; Thaddeus Kosciusko, a hero of the American Revolution who had been born in Poland; and Carl Schurz, a noted nineteenth-century political figure, born in Germany.

He liked to stroll around New York, pondering political problems of the day. He would often jot down his thoughts and observations on random slips of paper.

Schrank was easygoing and well-mannered and made a good impression on strangers. But he had no close relationships and never married. "I never had a friend in my life," he once wrote.

In 1904, when Schrank was 28, his uncle decided to retire. He turned the saloon over to Schrank, who kept it for only two years before selling it. After the sale, Schrank moved in with his aunt and uncle again, who had bought a tenement house in the Yorkville section of Manhattan. Schrank went to work for his uncle as the apartment handyman.

Schrank's aunt died in 1910. His uncle died the following year, leaving Schrank the apartment building. He couldn't quite support himself on his income as a landlord, so he worked part-time as a bartender. Because he didn't get along with his tenants, Schrank decided to move out of the tenement. Early in 1912, he rented a two-dollar-a-week room at a small hotel on Canal Street in Lower Manhattan.

Among the newspapers that Schrank read were the New York *Herald* and New York *World*. In 1912, both newspapers opposed Theodore Roosevelt and his efforts to win a third term as president. The papers never mentioned Roosevelt by name. Instead, they referred to him as "the Bull Moose," the "third-term candidate," or "the third-termer," an expression that Schrank liked to use.

September 14, 1912, was the eleventh anniversary of McKinley's death. Schrank sat in his hotel room writing a poem. In part, it read:

> Be a man from early to late;
> When you rise in the morning
> Till you go to bed,
> Be a man.
>
> If your country is in danger
> And you are called on to defend
> Where the battle is the hottest
> And death be the end,
> Face it and be a man.

As Schrank was writing, he claimed a strange thing happened. The ghost of McKinley appeared, touched him on the shoulder, and declared, "Let not a murderer take the presidential chair. Avenge my death!"

That was all the convincing that Schrank needed. Not long after his vision, he purchased a .38 caliber revolver at a gunshop near where he lived. He fashioned a makeshift holster for the weapon by slitting a hole in the bottom of his vest pocket. He slid the gun into the pocket and poked the barrel through the hole. The barrel was then hidden by the vest, while the pocket concealed most of the gun's handle. When Schrank put on his coat, no one noticed the bulge in his vest.

Schrank had read in the newspapers that Roosevelt was to speak in New Orleans on September 27, and he decided he would go there to carry out his mission. On September 21, Schrank boarded the liner *Comanche* in New York. The ship was bound for Charleston, South Carolina, and Jacksonville, Florida.

As the vessel steamed slowly south, Schrank got impatient and began to doubt whether he would get to New Orleans in time to confront Roosevelt. He left the ship in Charleston.

Schrank read local newspapers to keep track of Roosevelt. After New Orleans, the former president was planning to travel to Atlanta. Schrank took a train to Atlanta but arrived too late for Roosevelt's speech.

Schrank finally caught up with Roosevelt in Chattanooga, Tennessee. He waited in a crowd opposite the railroad station. When Roosevelt arrived and came out of the station to enter a car parked at the curb, Schrank stared at him in awe. He made no attempt to draw the pistol concealed in his vest pocket.

"I didn't shoot him in Chattanooga," Schrank said later, "because it was a new thing to me. I didn't exactly have courage to do it. . . ."

"Your nerve failed you?" he was asked.

"Just for a minute, it failed me, yes sir," he answered.

Roosevelt, not realizing, of course, that he was being hunted, returned to his home in Oyster Bay, New York. He resumed his campaigning early in October with a swing through the Midwest.

When the candidate arrived in Chicago on October 12 and attended a reception at the LaSalle Hotel, Schrank was there waiting. He was standing across the street from the hotel when Roosevelt pulled up in a chauffeured automobile. Once again Schrank did not shoot. "It would look awful bad if at the reception he would get shot down," said Schrank. He also felt he might get a better chance later.

The next day, a Sunday, Schrank took a train to Milwaukee, Wisconsin, where he knew Roosevelt was going to speak Monday night. He checked into a small hotel there, registering as "Walter Ross," and paid his bill in advance.

Monday afternoon, October 14, Roosevelt arrived in Milwaukee. That evening he was to deliver his speech at the Milwaukee Auditorium. Before the speech, Roosevelt attended a small dinner party that had been arranged in his honor at the Hotel Gilpatrick.

As news of the dinner spread throughout the city, hundreds of people gathered in the street outside the hotel, hoping to catch a glimpse of Roosevelt as he left for the auditorium. Schrank was one of those to hear of the dinner, and he had gotten to the hotel early, taking up a position near Roosevelt's open limousine. He waited quietly as darkness fell, occasionally fingering the revolver in his vest pocket.

Suddenly, a cheer went up from the crowd. Roosevelt had come out of the hotel. He strode across the sidewalk and climbed into the limousine. As Roosevelt stood in the car and waved to the crowd, Schrank put his right hand into his vest and pulled out the revolver, quickly aimed it between the heads of two men in front of him, and pulled the trigger.

Roosevelt felt a stab of pain in his chest. Stunned, he put out a hand to steady himself against the rear seat.

All hell broke loose. As Schrank fired, one of Roosevelt's aides, a former college football lineman, caught sight of the pistol. Before Schrank could fire again, the aide smashed him to the ground with a flying tackle. Others piled on and someone wrestled the gun from Schrank's grasp.

Schrank had fired from a distance of not more

A stunned Roosevelt in a photograph taken just after he was shot.

than six feet. Ordinarily, the bullet would have torn through Roosevelt's upper body, undoubtedly proving fatal. But the bullet first passed through his heavy overcoat and then through the metal case for his glasses that Roosevelt kept in his breast pocket. In the pocket, Roosevelt also carried his speech. It was one hundred pages long and it had been folded twice. The speech and the glasses case caused the bullet to lose much of its force. Had it not been for what he happened to be carrying in his breast pocket, Roosevelt would have been killed.

Metal case for his glasses and folded over speech helped save Roosevelt's life.

"He pinked me, Henry," is how Roosevelt described his injury to a friend. He did not feel it was serious enough to make him change his plans. He insisted that the driver proceed at once to the auditorium.

The audience had learned of the shooting and gave Roosevelt a thunderous greeting when he was introduced. There was blood on his shirt (and bullet holes in his speech) but Roosevelt managed to speak for fifty minutes. "It takes more than one bullet to kill a Bull Moose," he declared.

When some hecklers in the audience expressed doubt that he had been shot, Roosevelt immediately unbuttoned his vest to show his blood-stained shirt. Gasps of horror came from the audience.

At the end of the speech, Roosevelt was rushed to the hospital and treated for shock and loss of blood. Early the next morning, he was taken by train to Mercy Hospital in Chicago. It took him about a week to recover from the shooting.

An unsteady Roosevelt at the Milwaukee railroad station before boarding his train.

Doctors, however, never removed the bullet, feeling it was too risky to make an attempt. Roosevelt carried it in his chest until he died of natural causes in 1919.

When Roosevelt resumed campaigning after the shooting, he was cheered wildly at every appearance. The crowds chanted, "We want Teddy! We want Teddy!" But in the election that November, Roosevelt finished a distant second, not to President William Howard Taft, but to the Democratic candidate, Woodrow Wilson. Taft was third in balloting.

Schrank, found to be "suffering from insane delusions," spent the rest of his life in mental institutions in Wisconsin. When Theodore Roosevelt died, Schrank seemed saddened. "I am sorry to learn of his death," he said. "He was a great American. His loss will be a great one for the country."

In 1933, Theodore Roosevelt's cousin, Franklin D. Roosevelt, became president. He was reelected to a second term in 1936. Four years later, he announced he would try for a third term.

When Schrank found out, he became very disturbed. He told doctors that if he were free he would do something about it. He had saved the nation from a third-termer once, he explained, and he would not hesitate to do it again.

Schrank spent much of his time reading about politics and was not a troublesome patient. His health began to fail in 1940 and he died in 1943 (a year before Franklin Roosevelt ran for a *fourth* term). Schrank was sixty-seven years old when he died. His death came forty-two years to the day after his dream in which President McKinley sat up in his coffin and pointed an accusing finger at Theodore Roosevelt.

Although Franklin Roosevelt was easily elected when he ran for a third and then a fourth term, his break with tradition attracted wide opposition. In 1947, Congress proposed an amendment to the Constitution that put a limit on presidential terms of office. Within four years, it was ratified by three-fourths of the states. It says: "No person shall be elected to the office of the president more than twice . . ." It became the 22nd Amendment in 1951. John Schrank would have been glad.

6
Any President at All

Giuseppe Zangara, known as Joe, a short and dark-haired thirty-two-year-old bricklayer from Paterson, New Jersey, had visions of killing "a great ruler." It could be a king, prime minister, or president — anyone. Zangara didn't care.

It happened that "a great ruler" crossed Zangara's path in Miami, Florida, on the warm and breezy night of February 15, 1933. His name was Franklin D. Roosevelt. Roosevelt had trounced Republican Herbert Hoover in the national election the previous November and in eighteen days he was going to be inaugurated as the thirty-second president of the United States.

Looking tanned and rested, Roosevelt had arrived in Miami earlier in the evening aboard Vin-

Roosevelt was in good humor aboard Vincent Astor's yacht, a few hours before the attempt upon his life.

cent Astor's yacht *Nourmahal*, following a twelve-day fishing trip. He planned to make an informal speech that night in Miami's Bayfront Park.

After a brief press conference aboard the yacht, Roosevelt rode to the park in the backseat of a light blue open limousine. A car with Secret Service agents followed close behind.

Several thousand people awaited the president-elect at Bayfront Park. Most had taken seats in the huge amphitheater at the park's south end, where the president-elect was to speak. Plans called for Roosevelt to ride into the amphitheater and address the throng from his car.

When Roosevelt's car arrived, the crowd cheered loudly. The *rat-a-tat* of a drum and bugle corps filled the air. Roosevelt grinned and waved.

Joe Zangara, standing in a crowded aisle, watched as Roosevelt's car arrived. He was only twenty-five or thirty feet from the president-elect.

In his pocket, Zangara had a .32 caliber revolver he had purchased at a Miami pawnshop for eight dollars. The gun had a silver barrel and black handle. Zangara had loaded the gun with five bullets. Before the evening was over, he would use them all and each would find a target. Miraculously, Franklin Roosevelt escaped injury.

The attempt on Roosevelt's life was not the first time that Joe Zangara had tried to assassinate "a great ruler." Somewhere in Italy in 1922 or thereabouts, he had purchased a pistol with the idea of shooting King Victor Emmanuel III. The huge crowd that surrounded the King at the time interfered. The presence of the King's Royal Guard also helped Zangara to change his mind.

Guiseppe Zangara was born on September 7, 1900, in Ferruzzano, Italy, a small village in Calabria, a region at the very toe of the Italian boot. When he was two years old, his mother died. Not long after, his father remarried, choosing a woman with six daughters.

There was never enough money in the Zangara family, and when Guiseppe was six his father took him out of school so he could go to work. He

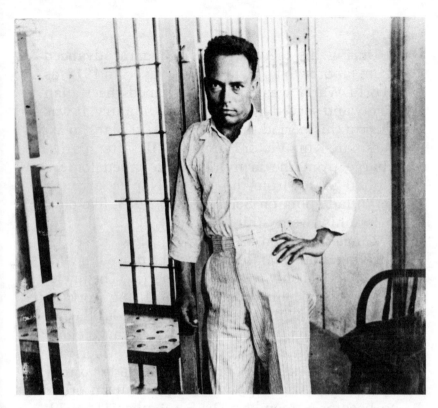

Joe Zangara, who attempted to assassinate Franklin Roosevelt.

became a laborer, shoveling dirt, swinging a pick, and doing other manual jobs.

Zangara's childhood caused him to be deeply bitter. He resented the fact that his father had taken him out of school at such a young age. He not only was angry at his father, but he also hated "capitalists," who, he believed, were responsible for his family's sad financial plight. All his life, he would feel deeply hostile to people who were better off or better educated than he was.

89

During his teenage years, Zangara advanced from laborer to apprentice bricklayer. In 1918, as World War I was ending, he joined the Italian Army and served five years in the infantry. It was during this period that Zangara laid plans to assassinate King Victor Emmanuel III. After his discharge from the army, Zangara sailed for the United States from the port of Naples, arriving in Philadelphia on September 2, 1923, five days before his twenty-third birthday.

Zangara settled in Paterson, New Jersey, a thriving industrial town, where he moved in with an uncle, his only relative in America. The uncle, a bricklayer, helped Zangara in getting work.

Almost immediately, Zangara filled out the papers necessary to become an American citizen. He had no great desire to become an American. But the bricklayers' union — which he didn't like — made him apply for citizenship in order to become a member. On September 11, 1929, Zangara became an American citizen.

Everything went smoothly for Zangara for several years. He earned good money. He bought nice clothes and a car. From time to time, he even sent money to his father back in Italy.

Those who worked with Zangara looked upon him as the "little guy." He was barely five feet tall. He weighed 106 pounds. He had thick black hair, dark eyes, a lean face, and a square jaw. Like more than a few of his co-workers, he spoke with a thick accent.

If there was anything unusual about Zangara, it was that he complained a lot about the privileges of the rich and how tough it was for the working man. But he never caused any trouble.

Another thing Zangara complained about was his stomach. He was in constant pain. Doctors were never able to determine its cause. Zangara himself believed the trouble stemmed from being made to work so hard at such a young age. "It spoil all my machinery — my stomach, all my insides," he once said. "Everything inside no good."

As he got older, Zangara led a more and more solitary life. He never went to the movies or had any interest in other forms of recreation. He never went out with women. When his uncle once suggested that he return to Italy to find himself a wife, Zangara instantly rejected the idea. He said he was too sick to think of getting married.

About the only thing he seemed to enjoy was a good game of checkers. He played well, but not with any special skill.

During the early 1930s, economic conditions began to change in the United States. It was the time of the Great Depression, triggered by the stock market's crash in October 1929. Workers lost their jobs and many families had no food. People by the thousands stood in bread lines to get food for their families. Farmers and city dwellers lost their homes.

Because of the Depression, Zangara could no

longer find steady work as a bricklayer. Then thirty-one years old, he started to travel. He decided he would go where there was lots of sunshine because warm weather made his stomach feel better. He visited Los Angeles, returned to New Jersey, tried Miami for a time, then went back to New Jersey again. In 1932, he left New Jersey for the last time, heading south.

He settled in Miami, eventually moving to an attic room in a boarding house in a rundown part of the city. His rent was two dollars a week.

Zangara was no longer interested in his work and had stopped looking for employment as a bricklayer. He lived off of his quickly dwindling savings. Once in a while, he was able to earn a few dollars showing tourists around Miami.

Some time during the winter of 1932–33, Zangara once again felt the need to kill "a great ruler." At the time, Herbert Hoover was president of the United States, but his term was drawing to a close. Soundly defeated in the election of 1932, Hoover was to step down in favor of Franklin Roosevelt on March 4, 1933.

"I was figuring to go to Washington — straight to Washington — to kill Hoover before Hoover go out," Zangara said later. Perhaps Zangara focused upon Hoover because he had come to identify him with the Depression and his own unhappiness.

But he never carried out the plan. Because of

the cold weather in Washington, he kept post-poning the trip.

Then one day in February he read that Roosevelt was planning to visit Miami. The article said that the president-elect would make a speech at Bayfront Park on the evening of February 15.

Roosevelt or Hoover — it didn't make any difference to Zangara. "I see Mr. Hoover first, I kill him first," he later admitted. "Make no difference. President just the same bunch — all same."

Zangara's plan to assassinate Roosevelt wasn't elaborate. He would go to the park early on the evening of the speech, get a seat in the front of the amphitheater, and shoot the president-elect at the first opportunity.

Zangara did get to the park early that evening — but not early enough. It was already dark when he arrived around eight o'clock. All the seats were filled and the aisles were beginning to get clogged with people.

He pushed and shoved his way down the aisle on the left side. When he got to within fifteen or twenty feet of the front row, a wall of people prevented him from going any farther.

Zangara heard a loud cheer go up from the crowd and guessed it was because Roosevelt had arrived. Since just about everyone around him was taller than he, Zangara's view of what was happening was blocked.

The limousine entered the park from behind the bandstand and drove around to the front. It came to a halt between the stage and the front row of audience seating. Another car followed with Secret Service men.

Floodlights picked out the president-elect, who was crippled by polio, as he boosted himself to a sitting position on the top edge of the car's rear seat. Someone handed him a small microphone. When the cheers and applause had died down, Roosevelt began to speak. His talk was short and friendly:

"I have had a very wonderful twelve days fishing in these Florida and Bahama waters. It has been a wonderful rest, and we have caught a great many fish. I am not going to attempt to tell you any fish stories, and the only fly in the ointment has been that I have put on about ten pounds."

Perched on the top of the seat, unable to move easily, and lit by bright spotlights, Roosevelt was a perfect target. But not for Zangara, who was buried in the crowd. He had to stand on tiptoe and peer over people's shoulders to see what was happening. There was no way he could aim his pistol.

When Roosevelt finished speaking, he handed back the microphone and slid down into the seat again. Doing so probably saved his life.

When he had entered the amphitheater, Roosevelt had noticed Mayor Anton J. Cermak of Chicago, with whom he was friendly, seated on the stage with a number of other dignitaries. After speaking, Roosevelt called out to Cermak, "Come

Perched atop the backseat of his limousine, Roosevelt addresses the crowd in Miami's Bay Front Park.

on down!" The mayor then joined several other wellwishers at the rear of Roosevelt's car. He and Roosevelt shook hands and chatted, and then the mayor started back for the stage.

Zangara had been waiting for the chance to shoot. Suddenly, it arrived. As the crowd was breaking up, benches were being vacated.

Zangara scrambled up on one of them and whipped out his pistol. Also standing on the bench was Mrs. Lillian Cross, forty-eight years old, the wife of a Miami physician. When Mrs.

Some people say that Mrs. Lillian Cross seized Zangara's arm as he was shooting at president-elect Roosevelt and probably saved his life.

Cross saw Zangara take out his pistol and point it toward Roosevelt, she was filled with horror. "Oh!" she said to herself, "he's going to kill the president."

As Zangara started to fire, one theory states that Mrs. Cross lunged for his arm, forcing the pistol upward. Although Mrs. Cross was clinging to his arm, Zangara fired five shots.

People screamed. Cermak staggered. Others who had been hit fell to the ground. A cop yelled, "Get Roosevelt out of here!"

Roosevelt, who could not walk without help, watched helplessly as police and Secret Service agents rushed Zangara, flinging him to the ground.

One of Zangara's bullets had struck Mayor Cermak in the right armpit and entered his right lung. Four other persons — two men and two women — were also hit.

Roosevelt's driver gunned the engine and his car started to move away. But Roosevelt protested, ordering the car to stop. "I'm all right! I'm all right! It's Tony!" he said. "Get Tony over here and drive to the hospital."

Secret Service agents carried the bloody Cermak to the car and placed him in the back seat next to Roosevelt. The president-elect cradled the wounded man in his arms all the way to the hospital. "Tony, keep quiet, don't move," Roosevelt said. "It won't hurt if you keep quiet and remain perfectly still."

"Thank God it wasn't you, Mr. President," Cermak said as the car raced through city streets.

In the days that followed, Mrs. Cross, who was so close to Zangara's pistol that she got gunpowder smudges on her face as he fired, was hailed for her heroism. Her actions may have prevented Zangara's bullets from finding their intended victim.

At first, Mayor Cermak seemed to be recovering, but then his condition worsened. On March 6, three weeks after the shooting and two days after Roosevelt had been inaugurated, the mayor died. The other victims recovered.

Zangara was first charged with assault in an attempt to assassinate the president. He pleaded guilty and was sentenced to eighty years in jail.

But upon Mayor Cermak's death, Zangara was retried. This time he was charged with murdering the mayor of Chicago. Again he pleaded guilty. Sentenced to death, he was electrocuted at the state prison in Raiford, Florida, on March 20, 1933, only thirty-three days after the shooting.

These three Miami police officers were credited with capturing Joe Zangara.

Zangara was defiant to the end. When a chaplain sought to comfort him, Zangara protested. "I want no minister," he said. "There's no God. It's all below."

Two guards sought to escort Zangara to the chair. He pulled away from them. "I go myself," he said to them. "I no scared of electric chair." To prove it, he strode up to the chair and sat down in it. "See, I no scared of electric chair," he repeated.

Suddenly, Zangara noticed there were no reporters or photographers present, and that angered him. From the day of his arrest, photographs of Zangara had appeared in the newspapers. There was no television in those days, but the newsreels, shown in movie theaters, had covered him thoroughly. Zangara had liked being the center of attention.

"Lousy capitalists!" he snarled. "No picture! No one here to take my picture. All capitalists a lousy bunch of crooks."

Guards strapped Zangara into the chair and placed a black hood over his head. He continued to talk as they made the final preparations.

"Go ahead," he told them. "Push the button."

Someone threw the switch and snuffed out Zangara's life.

Joe Zangara would have received much different treatment had his case been presented today. No effort was made at his trial to determine whether he was sane or insane. The defense did not call any psychiatrists to the witness stand to testify as to Zangara's mental condition. Practically everyone connected with the case agreed that he was sane, and that was that.

In 1953, when he was gathering material for a series of articles on presidential assassinations that appeared in *The New Yorker*, Robert J. Donovan interviewed a psychiatrist who had examined Zangara in jail two days after the shooting. "Medically, he was *not* sane," the psychiatrist told Donovan. Legally, he was considered sane in that he could recite the rules of behavior and he knew when he was acting contrary to those rules.

"I am sure," the psychiatrist continued, "that if he were alive today and we had the modern facilities for examining him psychiatrically, he would have been adjudicated as a very insane person and probably hopelessly insane."

Once Zangara pleaded guilty and was sentenced, no appeals were entered on his behalf. Zangara preferred to let justice take its course.

There's a footnote to the attempted assassination of president-elect Roosevelt. Some historians say that Mayor Cermak, not Roosevelt, was Zangara's intended victim. Cermak himself, from his hospital bed, was the first to put forth this theory. Judge John H. Lyle, a student of crime in Chicago, has said, "Zangara was a Mafia killer, sent from Sicily to do a job, and sworn to silence." (Judge Lyle's theory overlooks the fact that Zangara worked and lived in the United States for ten years before carrying out his assignment.)

Cermak had been elected as a "reform" mayor in Chicago. It was hoped that he would rid the city of gangsters. Cermak did wage war on the mob of criminals headed by Al Capone. But the mayor himself had a less than spotless reputation. He sought to replace Capone's gang with his own mobsters and was, in fact, known as "Ten Percent Tony," a reference to the amount of money he was believed to receive in kickbacks on city contracts and other deals.

Mayor Cermak had gone so far as to try to remove Frank Nitti, the man who had succeeded Capone after Capone went to prison. When the plan backfired, the frightened Cermak had fled Chicago on December 21, 1932, for an extended Florida vacation. This is why he was still there when president-elect Roosevelt arrived in mid-February the following year.

The theory that Cermak was Zangara's prime target has never been proved. Zangara himself always insisted that Roosevelt was the man he intended to kill. Of Cermak, he said, "I wasn't shooting at him, but I'm not sorry I hit him." Like Roosevelt, Hoover, and all the others, Cermak was just another "lousy capitalist."

7
Shootout at Blair House

President Lincoln was assassinated in a theatre. President Garfield was shot in a railroad station, and President McKinley was gunned down in a public exhibition hall. But Harry Truman was attacked at home. Truman, who became president in 1945 following the death of Franklin Roosevelt, is the only one of the nation's chief executives to come under assault in his Washington residence.

It wasn't the White House, however. The White House had been found to be structurally weak and even in danger of collapse, and was undergoing extensive repairs at the time. While the reconstruction was underway, President Truman and his wife and daughter lived in the elegant

President Truman was calm following the attempt upon his life. "A president has to expect those things," he said.

Blair House, diagonally across Pennsylvania Avenue from the White House. That is where the attack took place.

Wednesday, November 1, 1950, the day of the attack, was unseasonably warm in Washington. By two o'clock in the afternoon, the temperature had soared into the 80s.

The president, who continued to work in the White House's West Wing, spent a busy morning in his office. These were troubled times for the nation's chief executive. On June 25, 1950, communist forces from North Korea had invaded South Korea. Two days later, President Truman had announced that he was sending United States planes and ships to South Korea.

Later in the month, the president had ordered American ground forces to Korea. Truman realized, of course, his bold moves could easily trigger World War III. He later said that sending American troops to South Korea was the toughest decision of his political career.

After his morning working at the White House, the president was driven to Blair House for lunch. Following lunch, the sixty-six-year-old chief executive liked to nap, and the summerlike afternoon of November 1 was no exception. He went upstairs to lie down in his underwear. The Blair House doorman had instructions not to wake the president until two-thirty.

The president's schedule called for him to go to Arlington National Cemetery that afternoon to unveil a statue erected in the memory of Field Marshall Sir John Dill. A British member of the Combined Chiefs of Staff, Dill had died in Washington during World War II. The president was scheduled to leave for Arlington shortly before three o'clock.

While President Truman dozed peacefully, two Puerto Rican Nationalists, Oscar Collazo and Griselio Torresola, were getting ready to assassinate him. There was nothing complicated about their plan. They intended to go right up the front steps of Blair House and in the front door, blasting their way through police and Secret Service protection. Obviously, they were prepared to die for their cause.

Oscar Collazo and Griselio Torresola, both dark-haired and short in stature, had been born in Puerto Rico and now lived in New York City. Collazo, quiet and soft-spoken, was, at thirty-six, almost twelve years older than Torresola.

Collazo had left school after completing eighth grade. Torresola had dropped out after two years of high school. But both men were intelligent and informed. Collazo spent almost every spare moment reading newspapers, books on history, or political biographies.

Collazo and Torresola were loyal members of the Nationalist Party, whose goal was to win independence for Puerto Rico. They had both served as leaders of the party.

About the same time Collazo and Torresola were laying plans to attack Blair House, the Nationalist Party was staging a bloody revolt against government forces in Puerto Rico. In Penuelas, Ponce, Jayuya, Arecibo, and Utuado, Nationalist guerillas opened fire on police stations. They also attacked the governor's mansion in San Juan, the Puerto Rican capital. People were killed and wounded on both sides.

Torresola's brother and sister were deeply involved in the revolt. His sister, Doris, who was secretary to Pedro Campos, president of the Nationalist Party, was severely wounded in the fighting.

When Torresola learned what was happening, he wanted to go to Puerto Rico immediately to help out in the revolution. But when he told Collazo what he wanted to do, the older man had another idea. He told Torresola that they could be of greater help to their cause by going to Washington and staging some kind of a demonstration there. Collazo explained to Torresola that most Americans didn't even know where Puerto Rico was located, let alone understand the island's political history. In Washington, they would be able to attract attention to what the Nationalist Party was trying to accomplish.

As they continued to discuss the mission, Torresola agreed that going to Washington was a better idea than going to Puerto Rico. They decided the best way to get the publicity their cause needed was to attack the president, just as other members of the Nationalist Party had attacked the governor's mansion in San Juan.

On October 31, the two men purchased tickets on an afternoon train from Pennsylvania Station in New York to the nation's capital. They bought one-way tickets, not round-trip, perhaps because they realized their chances of ever returning to New York were very slim.

Neither Collazo nor Torresola had ever been to Washington before, so when they arrived early in

106

the evening, they decided to stay in the first hotel they saw, which was not far from the railroad station. They entered the hotel separately, pretending not to know one another. When they registered, they used fake names. Later that evening, they met in Collazo's room to study a map of Washington they had found in a hotel directory.

The next morning after breakfast, the two men, looking more like tourists than potential assassins, strolled about the grounds of the Capitol, which was within easy walking distance of their hotel. Then they decided to take a cab to Blair House to gather information for the attack.

Blair House has a rich history. A four-story structure made of yellow brick and stucco, Blair House was built in 1810 by Joseph Lovell, who later served as surgeon general of the Army. In the 1830s, it was purchased by Francis Preston Blair, one of President Jackson's closest advisers. He passed it on to his son, Montgomery Blair, who was President Lincoln's postmaster general. Except for the period that it was occupied by the Truman family — from November 21, 1948, to March 27, 1952 — Blair House has been used as the residence of distinguished White House visitors.

The sidewalk in front of Blair House is open to pedestrians, and hundreds of people pass by every day. Only a decorative iron picket fence about shoulder high separates the Blair House front yard from the sidewalk. A similar iron fence has been installed on each side of the concrete stairway leading to the front door.

When Collazo and Torresola arrived for their inspection tour, they noticed the flight of steps covered by a canopy. They also noticed guards on duty in white booths, not much bigger than telephone booths, that had been set up on the sidewalk at the east and west ends of the building.

After they had completed their tour, the two men returned to Collazo's hotel room. Both had brought .38 caliber pistols with them from New York. But Collazo, who had almost no experience with handguns, needed instruction in how to use his. Torresola was skilled in the use of firearms. He showed the older man how to insert an eight-bullet clip, how to eject it, and shove in another. He showed him how to aim and fire the weapon. The instruction session lasted about two hours.

Torresola gave Collazo three clips, each with eight bullets. He also gave him ten loose cartridges. Between them, Collazo and Torresola were armed with two revolvers and sixty-nine rounds of ammunition at the time they left their hotel for Blair House. It was shortly before two o'clock in the afternoon. President Truman, having finished lunch, was napping upstairs. Mrs. Truman and her mother, who was not well, were in another part of the house. The Trumans' daughter, Margaret, a concert singer, was in Portland, Maine, for a performance.

Leaving their hotel, Collazo and Torresola

hailed a cab and asked the driver to take them to the Treasury Building, which is on Pennsylvania Avenue a block and a half east of Blair House. "We had to study the way we were to approach Blair House," Collazo explained later. The two men walked west on Pennsylvania Avenue, with the White House on their left, Lafayette Park on their right. Just beyond the park was Blair House. They strolled past the house, trying to look as casual as possible. They realized the guards in the small guard booths loomed as their biggest problem. When they had passed the house, they turned around and walked back along Pennsylvania Avenue until they reached the Treasury Building again.

In their final discussion of tactics, Collazo and Torresola decided to launch a two-pronged attack. Torresola crossed to the south side of Pennsylvania Avenue, the side opposite Blair House. He walked west, past the White House, and past the Executive Office Building next to it. He then planned to recross the street and approach Blair House from the West.

Collazo, meanwhile, approached from the East along Pennsylvania Avenue, past Lafayette Park. He walked at a slower than normal pace since he had a shorter distance to cover than his partner, and they wanted to reach the front steps of Blair House at the very same time.

In front of Blair House at the moment Collazo and Torresola approached were three White

House policemen and a Secret Service agent. Leslie Coffelt of the White House police was seated in the west guard booth. Joseph Davidson, also a White House policeman, was posted in the east guard booth. Davidson was chatting with Floyd Boring, a Secret Service agent who was in charge of the detail that was later scheduled to accompany the president to Arlington Cemetery. A third White House policeman, Donald Birdzell, was beneath the canopy on the stairs leading to Blair House's front entrance.

As Collazo neared the house, he stopped, pulled his pistol from the waistband of his trousers, and aimed at Birdzell, who was turned away from him. But when Collazo pulled the trigger, nothing happened. Collazo had failed to release the safety lever, the device meant to prevent accidental firing of the weapon.

Frantically, Collazo fumbled with the weapon, trying to release the safety. Suddenly, the safety snapped and the gun went off accidentally, the bullet striking Birdzell in the right leg.

Birdzell hobbled out into Pennsylvania Avenue, stopped, turned, drew his revolver and began firing at Collazo, who had started up the stairs to the front door. Boring and Davidson went into action, too, firing at Collazo from the east guard booth.

Collazo fired back from a crouched position on the stairway. When he used up one clip of bullets, he quickly inserted a second clip. Boring and Davidson, both expert marksmen, were hindered by the iron stakes that formed the stairway fence. Some bullets were stopped by the fence; others were deflected. Yet one bullet nicked Collazo's ear, another clipped his nose, and a third went through his hat without touching his head.

Another Secret Service man now joined the fray. Vincent Mroz, emerging from a street level door at the east end of Blair House, also fired at Collazo, who eventually went down with a bullet in his chest, sprawling on the sidewalk in front of the stairway.

At the same time, Torresola was also blasting away. Approaching Blair House from the West, he dashed up to the west guard house booth, saw Coffelt inside, and opened fire on him, holding his revolver in both hands close to his chest. Coffelt went down, one bullet in his belly, another in his left side.

Torresola then spotted Joseph Downs, a White House police officer who was about to enter Blair House through the west basement door. Torresola fired three times and hit Downs with each shot. Downs collapsed.

Torresola saw Collazo under fire on the stairway and rushed to his aid. He noticed Birdzell firing at Collazo from the middle of Pennsylvania Avenue, and swung around and fired at the officer, hitting him in the left knee. Now wounded in both legs, Birdzell slumped to the ground.

Coffelt, despite his wounds — which were to

prove fatal — leaned against the doorway of the guard booth, took aim at Torresola as he was loading his revolver and sent a bullet through his brain. Torresola froze for a second, shook his head, then fell dead.

The fierce battle was over. It had lasted three minutes. Twenty-seven shots had been fired. One man was killed and another was dying. Three officers were wounded, but would recover.

The battle of Blair House. Gunmen approached Blair House from right and left along Pennsylvania Avenue. Lee House adjoins Blair House on the left.

President Truman, awakened by the gunfire, rushed to the window. He stared openmouthed at Collazo lying face downward on the sidewalk. When a guard saw Truman, he feared he might become a target of accomplices of the two assassins, and he yelled at him, "Get back! Get back!" The president was quick to obey.

Sirens screamed as police cars and ambulances began to arrive. Coffelt was rushed to the hospital, and died three hours and forty minutes later during emergency surgery. He and Torresola had killed one another.

Both Downs and Birdzell managed to survive. Collazo seemed seriously injured at first. But the bullet that had entered his chest was deflected by his breastbone. It passed through his right armpit and ended up in his right arm.

The attempt to assassinate the president in his official residence was foolish from beginning to end. Although both Collazo and Torresola caught the White House guards by surprise, they failed to penetrate even the first line of defense.

Unknown to Collazo and Torresola, a Secret Service agent was posted in a nearby office building with a clear view of Blair House. His assignment was to bring down any attacker who got as far as the front door. Even if Collazo and Torresola had been able to evade that man's fire and gotten through the front entrance, they would have faced an agent stationed inside who was armed with a submachine gun.

There was also an agent posted on the stairway leading to Truman's bedroom, another agent in front of his door, and still others in nearby rooms. According to one estimate, Collazo and Torresola would have had to shoot their way past at least twenty agents before reaching the president.

Later that day, President Truman demonstrated his faith in the Secret Service by going ahead with the plans to speak and unveil a statue at Arlington Cemetery. He acted as if nothing unusual had happened.

A White House police officer points to where bullet hit during the attack on President Truman. There is another hit in the bricks above the door, which is a side entrance to Blair House.

After he had recovered from his wounds, Collazo was brought to trial, charged with the murder of Leslie Coffelt. (Although it was bullets from Torresola's gun that had killed Collazo, the law provides that anyone who aids the principal offender shall be charged himself as a principal.) Collazo was also charged with assaulting Joseph Downs and Donald Birdzell "with the intent to kill," and with attempting to enter Blair House with the intention of killing the president.

Collazo pleaded not guilty and took the stand to say that he had not intended to kill the president or his guards. "I never had a feeling of hatred or dislike for Mr. Truman or any other American or anybody else . . ." he testified.

Collazo claimed he had come to Washington only to create "a demonstration" to advance the cause of Puerto Rican independence. It was Torresola who was to blame for the killings, according to the defense. He had acted like a crazed person in shooting and slaying Coffelt.

During his testimony, Collazo echoed some of the basic principles of the Nationalist Party. He blamed the United States for Puerto Rico's troubles. He believed, he said, that the United States had illegally seized Puerto Rico following the war with Spain in 1898. He shouted from the witness stand that American capitalists had exploited Puerto Rico for more than half a century.

"The economic conditions in Puerto Rico never

change," he said. "They are the same. It was bad before and it's bad today."

Collazo would not admit to any steps that had been taken to improve economic conditions. He seemed blind to all that President Truman had sought to do on behalf of Puerto Rico. In 1947, Congress had authorized the people of Puerto Rico to choose their own governor by popular election. President Truman had supported a new constitution and an improved form of government for Puerto Rico. The island would continue

White House police officer Leslie Coffelt was buried in Arlington National Cemetery in a military service attended by President and Mrs. Truman.

to be a part of the United States but as a self-governing commonwealth. The new constitution giving Puerto Rico commonwealth status was adopted in 1952.

It took the jury an hour and forty-five minutes to find Collazo guilty. When the judge asked Collazo whether he wanted to say anything before he was sentenced, Collazo said he did. He arose to speak in emotional terms about Puerto Rican independence. "Millions of people have been killed for liberty," he said, "and millions of people are dying right at this minute for liberty. In Korea, you have thousands of Puerto Ricans today fighting for the liberty of this country. They have no liberty themselves, but they are fighting for the liberty of the rest of the nations of the world.

"And where is the freedom of the Puerto Ricans? Could you answer me *that*? You don't know!"

Collazo was sentenced to be executed for the killing of Coffelt and for attempting to shoot his way into Blair House to attack the president. He had the privilege of asking the president for leniency, but he declined to do so, feeling it might somehow dishonor his cause.

Collazo was scheduled to be electrocuted on August 1, 1952. But just a week before, President Truman commuted Collazo's sentence to life imprisonment. On September 10, 1979, President Jimmy Carter, acting "for humane reasons," commuted Collazo's life sentence to time served, which provided for his immediate release. Once free, Collazo returned to Puerto Rico.

In October 1990, a reporter for *The New York Times* interviewed the seventy-five-year-old Collazo in San Juan, where he lived with his fifty-five-year-old daughter. As a result of a stroke he had suffered, Collazo's speech was slurred and he walked with a cane or used a wheelchair to get around. He had no regrets about what he had done or the fact that he had spent twenty-eight years in prison. He told the reporter: "A man, when he has convictions, has to be willing to sacrifice himself, and that's what I did."

8
Who Killed JFK?

In his hotel suite in Fort Worth, Texas, on the morning of the day he died, John F. Kennedy sipped coffee and discussed the hazards a president faces when he makes personal appearances. His special assistant, Kenny O'Donnell, remembered what the president said and later repeated his words to a panel of investigators. "If anybody really wanted to shoot the president of the United States, it would not be a difficult job — all you have to do is get on a high building someday with a telescopic sight," Kennedy declared.

A few hours after the president made his observation, he lay dead in a Dallas hospital, shot in the head by a killer armed with a telescope-equipped rifle, shooting from the window of a tall building.

The youngest man ever elected president, Kennedy was also the youngest to die in office. Besides his youth, he had strength, energy, and good looks. He seemed to be guided by the principle that all problems can be solved. One newspaper called him "the golden boy."

Kennedy's murder, which came two years and ten months after his inauguration, shocked the world. At U.S. military bases from Germany to

President Kennedy with son, John Jr., and daughter, Caroline, in the Oval Office on Halloween, just a few weeks before he was assassinated.

South Korea, artillery pieces boomed out every half hour from dawn to dusk, a salute to the nation's fallen leader. In countries around the world, the streets in front of U.S. embassies were jammed with mourners. Some stood in line for hours to write their names in books of condolence.

In the United States, the three major television networks used virtually every camera and reporter to cover the story. All regular programming and all commercials were suspended for three days, or until after Kennedy's funeral and burial on Monday, November 25.

Millions sat glued to their TV sets and watched the tragic story unfold. The images were unforgettable: the scene inside the warehouse where the killer had knelt and tracked the president; Jacqueline Kennedy, her suit and stockings stained with her husband's blood, a guardian at the side of his bronze casket arriving at Andrews Air Force Base outside Washington; Lyndon Johnson, Kennedy's vice president, speaking his first words as president; Caroline, the president's daughter, almost six years old, brushing a tear from her eye following the funeral service; John Jr., the president's son, whose third birthday was the day of his father's funeral, saluting the casket.

The man who killed Kennedy was twenty-four-year-old Lee Harvey Oswald, who worked as a $1.25-an-hour order-filler at the Texas School Book Depository. His job gave him access to a sixth floor window that provided a perfect vantage point for the shooting.

Oswald was a social misfit, a lifelong loner. Born in New Orleans in 1939, his school and military records disclose emotional difficulty. He dropped out of high school at seventeen and joined the Marine Corps. He qualified as a "sharpshooter" on the rifle range and got trained as an electronics-equipment operator. He applied for and got a discharge in 1959. A month later he

This snapshot of Lee Harvey Oswald was taken by his wife, Marina.

went to the Soviet Union. He wanted to become a Soviet citizen but was turned down. He returned to the United States in 1962 with his Soviet-born wife, Marina, and their baby daughter.

Oswald was no stranger to law enforcement agencies. Because he had rejected the United States in favor of the Soviet Union, he was known to the Federal Bureau of Investigation. The F.B.I. was aware, in fact, that Oswald was working at the Texas School Book Depository.

A few months before the assassination, on August 9, 1963, Oswald had been arrested and fined $10 for disturbing the peace. The charge was the result of a scuffle in which he had been involved while passing out leaflets in New Orleans for the Fair Play for Cuba Committee, an organization that supported Cuban dictator Fidel Castro. Soon after, Oswald took his family to Dallas and got the job in the warehouse.

What was Oswald's motive in killing Kennedy? Did he act out of hatred for American society? Was he seeking a place in history, a role as a "great man"? Nobody knows, and he was killed before he got a chance to say.

More than thirty years after the deadly gunshots, investigators and the public are still puzzling over the facts surrounding the president's murder. Many people believe there was a conspiracy, or at least a second gunman. The Mafia, the Cuban government, the Soviet Union, the Central Intelligence Agency, and the Federal Bureau of Investigation have all been linked to the assassination at one time or another. More than 600 books have been written about the assassination. Scores of TV documentaries, miniseries, and Hollywood feature films have been produced on the topic. And it does not seem likely the flow is ever going to stop.

John Kennedy was elected in 1960 by the thinnest of margins, edging out Republican Richard Nixon by less than a quarter of a million votes among the almost seventy million ballots cast. But once he took office, Kennedy received the support of most Americans. They admired his style, energy, wit, and self-confidence. He and his wife and the two young children brought youth and sparkle to the White House.

During the thirty-four months and two days he served as president, the Cold War raged, dealing Kennedy tough challenges from the Soviet Union in Cuba, Berlin, and elsewhere. On the domestic front, the nation enjoyed great prosperity. But most of Kennedy's hopes went unfulfilled, not to be realized until the Johnson administration.

During the summer of 1963, Kennedy looked forward to being re-elected the next year. He felt if he could be returned to the White House with wide support, he would be better able to develop solutions to the nation's problems.

Kennedy's trip to Texas in November was strictly political, made with votes in mind. He wanted to smooth over splits among Texas Democrats, to make fund-raising appearances for the party, and to be seen by the public. Five cities — San Antonio, Houston, Fort Worth, Dallas, and Austin — were to be visited.

The Secret Service were not pleased with the choice of Dallas, for the city had been the scene of several violent incidents, triggered by bigotry and hatred. During the 1960 campaign for the presidency, Texas Senator Lyndon Johnson, the Democratic candidate for vice president, and his wife had been cursed and spat upon by a mob in a hotel lobby. In the spring of 1963, swastikas had been painted above Dallas stores owned by Jews.

On October 24 that year, a month before the presidential visit, Adlai Stevenson , the U.S. ambassador to the United Nations, had been spat upon by and struck with a sign after a speech in the Dallas Memorial Auditorium. Some protestors in the audience had burst into an aisle yelling, "Kennedy will get his reward in hell!"

Stevenson told one of Kennedy's aides of the hostile feelings in Dallas and said perhaps the president should not visit the city. But later Stevenson realized that if the president canceled the trip it would look like he was trying to dodge his critics.

The trip went on as scheduled. Late on the morning of November 21, the president and his wife said goodbye to their children and boarded the presidential airplane, Air Force One, at Andrews Air Force Base in Maryland. San Antonio was the first stop for the presidential party, where they were greeted by large and enthusiastic crowds.

After the president spoke at Brooks Air Force Base, he and Mrs. Kennedy flew to Houston. There they received another warm welcome. In the evening Kennedy delivered another speech, after which he and his wife reboarded Air Force One for a flight to Fort Worth. The couple spent the night in the Texas Hotel in Forth Worth.

That same day, Thursday, November 21, 1963, Lee Harvey Oswald, at work as a shipping clerk at the Texas School Book Depository in Dallas, approached a co-worker, Wesley Frazier, and asked a favor. After work that day, Oswald wanted to hitch a ride with Frazier out to Irving, about twelve miles away, to the home of Mrs. Ruth Paine, where his wife and two baby daughters were staying. Oswald himself was living in a rooming house in Dallas. He explained he wanted to pick up some "curtain rods" to use in his room — which already had curtains and curtain rods. Frazier agreed to give him a lift.

Earlier in the year, Oswald had purchased a cheap 6.5 mm. Mannlicher-Carcano Italian Army rifle with a powerful telescopic sight from a Chicago mail order firm. In making the purchase, Oswald had used the name "A. Hidell." He stored the weapon, wrapped in an old blanket, in the garage behind the Paine house.

Oswald stayed overnight at Mrs. Paine's. The next morning, while everyone else in the house was still asleep, Oswald arose, made himself a cup of coffee, and went out to the garage. When he came back to the house, he was carrying a package wrapped in brown paper that was about the size of a rifle. He took the package with him that morning when he left to meet Wesley Frazier for the trip back to Dallas. He placed the package on the backseat of the car, explaining it contained the curtain rods.

When they reached the parking lot at the Book Depository, Oswald hopped out of the car ahead of Frazier. Tucking the long package under one arm, Oswald hurried into the building.

Oswald had picked out a window on the sixth floor from which he planned to shoot. From his perch, he knew he would be able to see the motorcade approaching, then watch it directly below as the cars made a sweeping left turn and headed down a sloping roadway toward an underpass and freeways. It was a bird's eye view.

On Friday, November 22, the president arose early and put on a gray suit, striped shirt, and blue tie. After breakfast, he addressed a crowd of several thousand behind barricades in a parking lot across the street from the hotel. Someone in the throng yelled, "Where's Jackie?" Kennedy broke into laughter. "Mrs. Kennedy is organizing herself," he said with a grin. "It takes longer, but, of course, she looks better than we do when she does it." The crowd roared.

Later in the morning, the president addressed a breakfast sponsored by the Fort Worth Chamber of Commerce. When Mrs. Kennedy appeared, the audience got to its feet. She was wearing a pink tailored wool suit and a matching pillbox hat. When he introduced her, the president said, "Two years ago I introduced myself in Paris by saying that I was the man who had accompanied Mrs. Kennedy to Paris. I am getting that same sensation as I travel around Texas." The crowd loved it.

After breakfast, the president and Mrs. Kennedy made the short trip from Fort Worth to Love Field in Dallas aboard Air Force One. A crowd of five thousand was there to greet them. Mrs. Kennedy was welcomed by a committee that gave her a bouquet of red roses.

In the fifteen-car motorcade that had been assembled, the Kennedys and Governor and Mrs. Connally were to ride in a dark blue 1961 Lincoln convertible equipped with a clear plastic protective bubble. But because the early morning clouds had lifted and the day had turned warm and sunny, a presidential aide said the bubble was not to be used. The president himself ordered that no Secret Service agents were to "ride the bumper," that is stand on the small running boards attached to the rear of the car.

By the most direct route, it was four miles to

Huge crowds greeted the Kennedys in Dallas. The president and his wife sat in the rear seat of the limousine, and Governor Connally and his wife in the car's jump seats.

the Trade Mart, where the president was to make a luncheon address, from Love Field. But the route that had been laid out called for the motorcade to meander for about ten miles through the suburbs and the city.

The newspapers in Dallas carried diagrams showing the route of the procession of automobiles. While the first reports indicated the motorcade might not get very close to the Texas School Depository, later editions reported it would enter Dealey Plaza, turning down Houston

Street, then left on Elm Street, directly in front of the Depository. The motorcade would then proceed slightly downhill on Elm Street, which angled away from the building. It was from the newspapers that Lee Harvey Oswald learned that his victim would be delivered to him, at his place of work.

By noontime, a warm sun was shining. Dallas police chief Jesse Curry was at the wheel of the motorcade's lead car. Behind came the big blue Lincoln, with its presidential flags on the front fenders. The president sat in the rear seat on the right. Mrs. Kennedy was beside him on the left, Governor Connally sat in a jump seat directly in front of the president, while Mrs. Connally was in a jump seat in front of Mrs. Kennedy. Two Secret Service agents occupied the front seat, one of whom served as the driver.

Just behind the presidential car came four motorcycles. Next came another open car full of Secret Service agents, then another open car with Vice President Johnson and his party. The rest of the cars and three press buses were stretched out behind for almost half a mile.

On the drive into Dallas, the president twice ordered his car to stop. At Craddock Park, he spotted a homemade sign held by boys and girls. It read: MR. PRESIDENT, PLEASE STOP AND SHAKE OUR HANDS. The president leaned forward between Governor and Mrs. Connally and said to the driver, "Let's stop here."

Once the car had eased to a stop, the president leaned out and shook dozens of little hands. "Our sign worked! It worked!" said one of the boys. The Secret Service men on the car behind jumped off the running boards where they had been riding and made the children get back to the curb. The motorcade started again.

The president ordered the car stopped a second time when he saw a nun in a black habit on a corner with a group of small children. He reached out to her, smiled, and spoke a few words. Then the cars moved on.

The crowds along the route were large and friendly. The president smiled and waved. "Thank you. Thank you," he kept saying in a soft voice. Mrs. Kennedy smiled and waved, too.

When the motorcade reached the downtown area, the huge crowd there roared a loud welcome. In some places, the people stood a dozen deep at the curbs. The president was plainly pleased. Children held signs that said HOORAY FOR JFK. Confetti floated down from tall buildings.

As the motorcade came to the end of the business district and into Dealey Plaza, the cars began a series of turns that would lead directly to the Trade Mart. The crowds were thinner. The president's car turned right on Houston Street for one block, traveling toward Elm at precisely 11.2 miles an hour. Ahead loomed the Texas School Book Depository. A Hertz-Rent-a-Car sign atop the building flashed 12:29 in electric lights.

In his sixth floor window, Lee Harvey Oswald watched silently. The president's car was coming directly toward him.

In his hands, Oswald cradled his 6.5 mm Mannlicher-Carcano Italian Army rifle with its four-power telescopic sight. He knew that once he sighted the president in the crosshairs, Kennedy, at four hundred feet, would appear to be only one hundred feet away. One shell was in the rifle's chamber. Three more were in the clip below, ready to be snapped into place.

No one can say for certain why Oswald, at this instant, did not bring the rifle to his shoulder, take aim, and fire. Perhaps he figured that at the sound of the gunfire, the Secret Service agents in the cars behind the president would look up and spot him in the window. Oswald decided to be patient, to wait a few more seconds. The motorcade would then have turned onto Elm Street and be heading away from him. The president would then be even more of an exposed target. And Oswald would not feel as vulnerable to return fire from the Secret Service agents.

Oswald watched as the presidential car eased into Elm Street just below his window and, still moving slowly, started heading down a curving hill toward the railroad underpass and the expressway leading to the Trade Mart.

Inside the Lincoln, Mrs. Connally turned toward Kennedy. "Mr. President," she said, "you can't say Dallas doesn't love you."

"No," the president replied, "you sure can't."

It was 12:30. Oswald raised the rifle to his shoulder and fixed the president's head in the crosshairs. He squeezed the trigger. Kennedy was waving to the crowd when the shot rang out.

The bullet hit the branch of a live oak tree and ricocheted into the pavement near the rear of the car, causing chips of concrete to spray upward. The sharp sound drew gasps from many in the crowd. "What was that?" people asked one another.

To some it sounded like a firecracker. Others thought a car had backfired. But Governor Connally, a hunter, knew it was no firecracker or backfire. He knew the sound of a rifle when he heard it. Mrs. Kennedy, not sure of the sound, turned toward her husband.

Oswald, in the window, quickly worked the bolt action of the rifle. The car was an easier target now, with no branches to interfere. He got a bead on the president's head and fired.

The bullet hit the president in the upper back, just below the neck, and cut through to exit from his throat. Tumbling over and over, it struck Connally on the right side of his back, tore open his chest, splintered a rib, and exited below his right nipple. It then shattered his right wrist and was deflected downward, wounding him in the left thigh.

The governor felt like he had been punched in the back. His wife pulled him down into her lap. The president, putting both hands toward his neck, slumped toward his wife.

"We're hit!" said a Secret Service agent in the front seat. The driver slammed on the brakes and the car veered to the right and almost stopped.

Mrs. Kennedy was staring at her husband when a third bullet from Oswald's rifle struck Kennedy in the back of the head. A woman standing at the curb screamed, "My God! He's shot!"

President Kennedy slumps into the arms of his wife, Jacqueline, after being hit by a bullet.

Spewing blood from his big head wound, Kennedy lurched backward and to the left. "Oh, my God!" Mrs. Kennedy gasped, "They've killed my husband! Jack! Jack!"

The car jerked forward and began to pick up speed. Mrs. Kennedy climbed out onto the lid of the trunk, apparently to give a hand to Secret Service agent Clint Hill who was running toward the presidential car from the car behind. Once Hill was aboard, he pushed Mrs. Kennedy back into her seat. As the car raced to Parkland Memorial Hospital, Mrs. Kennedy held the president in her arms.

Orders were flashed to Parkland Hospital to be ready to receive the wounded president and governor. The hospital medical team saw at once that the right half of the president's brain had been shot away, and there was no hope of survival. It is almost certain that Oswald's third shot had killed him outright. The president was pronounced dead at 1 PM and Lyndon Johnson was quickly sworn in. Governor Connally recovered from his wounds.

As television and radio carried the news of the president's death to a shocked world, the search for his killer was underway. There was no doubt as to where the shots had come from. In the second car behind Lyndon Johnson's car, Mrs. Earle Cabell, wife of the mayor of Dallas, had seen a "projection" sticking out of a window of the

Lyndon Johnson is sworn in as president in the cabin of Air Force One. Jacqueline Kennedy stands to his right and his wife, Lady Bird Johnson, to his left.

School Book Depository. Bob Jackson, a photographer for a Dallas newspaper, riding in a press car at the rear of the motorcade, had seen a rifle being drawn back through an open window. Directly across from the School Book Depository, Amos Lee Euins, fifteen years old, a ninth-grade student, had seen a man shoot twice from a window. Frightened, Euins had hid behind a bench.

At the moment the shots rang out, Roy Truly, superintendent of the School Book Depository, had been standing in front of the building to watch the president pass. Suddenly, someone in the crowd pointed to an upper floor and shouted, "Someone up there has a gun."

Truly and a policeman raced up the stairway. On the second floor they came upon Oswald near a Coke machine. "Do you know this man?" the policeman asked, pointing his gun at Oswald. "Yes," Truly answered. "He works for me." Satisfied, the two men turned and continued up the stairs.

Oswald slipped out of the building and boarded a bus bound for the Oak Cliff section of Dallas, where he lived. When the bus got held up in traffic, Oswald got off and took a cab to the boarding house. In his room, he put on a zippered jacket and stuffed a .38 caliber pistol into his belt. He also took several .38 caliber cartridges. His landlady later recalled she had never seen him move so fast.

At around 1:15 that afternoon, Patrolman J. D. Tippit spotted Oswald and called him over to his patrol car. A description of the president's assassin had been broadcast to the police after a check of employees at the School Book Depository showed Oswald to be missing. Oswald walked over to the window on the passenger side of the car, leaned in, and spoke to the officer. When Tippit got out and started toward the front of the car, Oswald pulled out his revolver and shot him four times.

Oswald fled the scene in panic. One witness to the shooting heard Oswald mutter either "poor damn cop" or "poor dumb cop." Another witness reported the killing to police headquarters. Sirens began to scream throughout the neighborhood.

Oswald ducked into the entrance of a shoe store when a police car approached. Then, as the salesman in the shoe store watched, Oswald hurried down the street and, without buying a ticket, darted into the Texas Theatre where *War Is Hell* was playing. The shoe salesman, who had become suspicious, alerted the theatre cashier, who called the police.

When the police arrived, they entered the theatre and turned on the lights. The shoe salesman pointed out Oswald. Patrolman M. N. McDonald approached him and said, "Well, it's all over now." Oswald jumped up and hit McDonald in the face, then drew his pistol. But the police overpowered him before he could fire.

In police custody, Oswald was defiant. At first he was charged with the murder of Officer Tippit, and later with the assassination of the president. He denied both charges over and over.

But the evidence against Oswald convinced authorities that it was he who had fired the three shots. Within minutes after the assassination, police found the Mannlicher-Carcano rifle hidden on the sixth floor of the Book Depository. They also found three cartridge cases.

The FBI learned the same rifle had been mailed in March 1963 from a Chicago company to "A. Hidell, P.O. Box 2915" in Dallas. Handwriting experts determined that the coupon used to order the weapon, the signature on the money order to pay for it, and the address on the envelope were written in Oswald's hand. Oswald's wallet contained identification cards for "Alek James Hidell."

Oswald's palm print was found on the rifle. Some cotton fibers — blue, gray-black, and orange-yellow — were found clinging to the rifle butt. Under a microscope, the fibers were found to match the fibers of the three-color shirt that Oswald was wearing on the day of the assassination.

Oswald's wife, Marina, was later to identify the weapon as the "fateful rifle of Lee Oswald." In the spring of 1963, she had taken a backyard snapshot of her husband posing with the rifle. She said he liked to practice using the bolt mechanism and to peer through the crosshairs in the telescopic sight.

After the assassination, police found a paper bag on the floor near the window through which the shots had been fired. It was the bag in which Oswald's "curtain rods" had been wrapped. Oswald's palm print and a fingerprint were on the paper.

Six eyewitnesses identified Oswald at the Tippit murder scene or running away from the scene, gun in hand. Ballistics tests showed the bullets in Tippit's body were fired from Oswald's revolver.

All available evidence pointed to Lee Harvey Oswald as the lone gunman who had assassinated the president. No evidence came to light involving anyone else in the shooting.

On Sunday, Dallas police were getting ready to transfer Oswald from police headquarters to the county jail. The plan was to escort the prisoner past a throng of reporters and TV cameramen to a vehicle waiting in the basement garage. The police even announced the time of the transfer in advance.

As Oswald, his face swollen and bruised from his scuffle with police at the time of his capture, was being taken through the basement, Jack Ruby, a fifty-year-old Dallas night club operator, slipped through the crush of reporters. When Oswald got near, Ruby drew a .32 caliber pistol and shot the accused assassin in the belly. Millions watched the shooting on television.

Oswald was rushed to Parkland Memorial Hospital, the same hospital where the president had been brought just two days before. Some of the same doctors who had tried to save the president's life also worked on Oswald. But their efforts were in vain. Oswald died at 1:07 PM, forty-eight hours and seven minutes after the president had been pronounced dead.

The Dallas police were denounced for allowing so valuable a prisoner to be so easily shot. Many people found it hard to believe the police could have been so careless. Some began to speculate the police may have been involved in the murder of President Kennedy or an effort to cover up the identity of the real killer.

In explaining why he had killed Oswald, Jack Ruby said he was deeply disturbed by the murder of the president and what Kennedy's loss meant to his widow and their children. "I couldn't forget how Jackie had suffered, and that Caroline and John wouldn't have a daddy anymore," Ruby said.

Ruby was jailed and charged with murder. If found guilty, he faced a death sentence.

On Sunday, the same day Oswald was shot, President Kennedy's casket was taken to the rotunda of the Capitol to lie in state surrounded by a military honor guard. Tens of thousands filed past the coffin. Some people waited in line for seven or eight hours.

Funeral services were held the next day at Saint Matthew's Cathedral. A million people lined the streets of Washington as the president's casket, carried by a caisson pulled by six matched gray horses, was borne from the White House to the church. Immediately behind the caisson came the traditional riderless horse. A sword hung from its black saddle. A pair of boots were reversed in the

141

KENNEDY IS KILLED BY SNIPER AS HE RIDES IN CAR IN DALLAS; JOHNSON SWORN IN ON PLANE

TEXAN ASKS UNITY

Congressional Chiefs of 2 Parties Give Promise of Aid

By FELIX BELAIR Jr.
Special to The New York Times

WASHINGTON, Nov. 22—Lyndon B. Johnson returned to a stunned capital this evening to assume the duties of the Presidency.

"This is a sad time for all people. We have suffered a loss that cannot be weighed. For me it is a deep personal tragedy. I know the world shares the sorrow that Mrs. Kennedy and her family bear. I will do my best. That is all I can do. I ask for your help—and God's."—President Lyndon Baines Johnson.

PRESIDENT'S BODY WILL LIE IN STATE

Funeral Mass to Be Monday in Capital After Homage Is Paid by the Public

By JACK RAYMOND
Special to The New York Times

WASHINGTON, Saturday, Nov. 23—The body of John F. Kennedy will lie in state in the East Room of the White House until Monday.

PARTIES' OUTLOOK FOR '64 CONFUSED

Republican Prospects Rise —Johnson Faces Possible Fight Against Liberals

By WARREN WEAVER Jr.
Special to The New York Times

WASHINGTON, Nov. 22—President Kennedy's assassination is certain to throw the American political scene into turmoil today.

LEFTIST ACCUSED

Figure in a Pro-Castro Group Is Charged— Policeman Slain

By GLADWIN HILL
Special to The New York Times

DALLAS, Saturday, Nov. 23—Lee Harvey Oswald, a 24-year-old warehouse work r who once lived in the Soviet Union, was charged late last night with assassinating President Kennedy.

John Fitzgerald Kennedy
1917-1963

Why America Weeps

Kennedy Victim of Violent Streak He Sought to Curb in the Nation

By JAMES RESTON
Special to The New York Times

WASHINGTON, Nov. 22—America wept tonight, not alone for its dead young President, but for itself.

City Goes Dark

By ROBERT C. DOTY

Gov. Connally Shot; Mrs. Kennedy Safe

President Is Struck Down by a Rifle Shot From Building on Motorcade Route— Johnson, Riding Behind, Is Unhurt

By TOM WICKER
Special to The New York Times

DALLAS, Nov. 22—President John Fitzgerald Kennedy was shot and killed by an assassin today.

He died of a wound in the brain caused by a rifle bullet that was fired at him as he was riding through downtown Dallas in a motorcade.

Vice President Lyndon Baines Johnson, who was riding in the third car behind Mr. Kennedy's, was sworn in as the 36th President of the United States 99 minutes after Mr. Kennedy's death.

Mr. Johnson is 55 years old; Mr. Kennedy was 46.

Shortly after the assassination, Lee H. Oswald, who once defected to the Soviet Union and who has been active in the Fair Play for Cuba Committee, was arrested by the Dallas police. Tonight he was accused of the killing.

Suspect Captured After Scuffle

THE NEW PRESIDENT: Lyndon B. Johnson takes oath before Judge Sarah T. Hughes in plane at Dallas. Mrs. Kennedy and Representative Jack Brooks are at right. To left are Mrs. Johnson and Representative Albert Thomas.

WHEN THE BULLETS STRUCK: Mrs. Kennedy moving to the aid of the President after he was hit by a sniper yesterday in Dallas. A guard mounts rear bumper. Gov. John B. Connally Jr. of Texas, also in the car, was wounded.

The front page of The New York Times, November 23, 1963.

stirrups — a sign that a commander had fallen and would never ride again.

Behind the slow moving caisson and riderless horse walked Mrs. Kennedy, with the president's brother, Robert, at her side, and the other members of the president's family.

They were followed by President Johnson and his wife. A limousine carrying Caroline and John was next.

Then, filling the street from one curb to the other, came an army of world leaders. They represented more than ninety countries. At the front and center marched French President Charles de Gaulle. At his side was Queen Frederika of Greece. Those on either side of them included King Baudouin of Belgium, Emperor Haile Selassie of Ethiopia, and West German's President Heinrich Lubke.

After the funeral Mass at Saint Matthew's, Kennedy's body was taken to Arlington National Cemetery across the Potomac River for burial. Mrs. Kennedy lighted an "eternal flame" to burn over the president's gravesite, which is now visited annually by millions.

In the months that followed the tragedy, countless public buildings and geographic sites were named for President Kennedy. President Johnson ordered the National Aeronautics and Space Administration's huge complex in Florida to be named the John F. Kennedy Center. New York City named its biggest airport in his honor. Con-

Three-year-old John F. Kennedy, Jr., salutes the caisson bearing the casket of his father. Standing behind him are his sister, Caroline, six years old on November 27; his mother, Jacqueline; and his uncle, Robert.

Crowds fill the sidwalks to watch Kennedy's funeral procession in Washington. The horse-drawn caisson bearing the body is followed by the riderless horse.

gress voted funds for the John F. Kennedy Center for the Performing Arts in Washington, D.C.

Even as the nation grieved for its murdered president, questions began to be asked about the assassination and the events surrounding it. Many people found it hard to believe that Lee Harvey Oswald, a social failure, a Marine with a dishonorable discharge, a sulky book clerk, could, acting alone, snuff out the life of the president of the United States. He must have had an accomplice, or several of them, it was said. Or perhaps Oswald was part of a vast conspiracy, a secret plot formulated by a hostile foreign government.

Lyndon Johnson moved quickly to still the rumors. On November 29, 1963, just seven days after he became president, Johnson issued Executive Order 11130, setting up a commission to investigate every aspect of the assassination. To head the commission, Johnson called upon Chief Justice Earl Warren, one of the most respected Americans of the time. He was known for his leadership in breaking down the barriers of racial discrimination through landmark Supreme Court decisions.

The Warren Commission, as it came to be called, spent ten months interviewing more than five hundred witnesses and reviewing hundreds of documents. The FBI, CIA, the Secret Service, and the State Department helped out. The commission produced a twenty-six volume report, which, with its seven-hundred-page summary, takes up more shelf space than the World Book Encyclopedia.

But the Warren Report, released in September 1964, contained no unexpected news. It said Lee Harvey Oswald fired all three shots at President Kennedy from the sixth floor of the Texas School Book Depository overlooking Dealey Plaza. The report also stated there was "no evidence that anyone assisted Oswald in planning or carrying out the assassination."

146

In the years after, the Warren Report was widely criticized. It was said that in its haste to get the report out, the commission made errors and omitted important information from the CIA, information that could have linked the agency with Kennedy's murder.

The same year the Warren Report was made public, Jack Ruby was found guilty of the murder of Lee Harvey Oswald. The verdict was reversed two years later on the grounds that the judge had allowed illegal testimony. A new trial was ordered. But Ruby, suffering from cancer, died in 1967 before a new trial could begin.

With Ruby's death, new conspiracy theories began to be heard. One claimed that Ruby was a Mafia gunman, although he had never confessed to having any part in a conspiracy.

With more and more critics denouncing the Warren Report, Congress acted. During the 1970s, the House Select Committee on Assassinations began re-investigating the Kennedy slaying. The committee, which published its twenty-nine volumes of findings in 1979, agreed with the Warren Commission that it was Oswald who fired three shots at the president. Two shots hit and one missed.

The committee did raise doubts about Oswald being the lone gunman, however. After listening to audio tapes taken from the radio of a police motorcycle in Dealey Plaza, the committee concluded there was a second gunman who fired a fourth shot. But the evidence was later disproved by the Committee of Acoustics of the National Research Council, which said the sound of the fourth shot was probably just radio static.

Many of the people who criticize the Warren Report and the findings of the House Committee on Assassinations believe that a second gunman was involved in the assassination. They question whether Oswald could have fired his rifle fast enough to get off three shots. They also cannot accept the fact that the same bullet that hit Kennedy in the neck also wounded Governor Connally, damaging both a rib and his wrist, and ending up embedded in his left thigh. They call it the "magic bullet."

There is, however, a good deal of independent evidence to support the government's findings. Dr. John K. Lattimer of the Columbia Presbyterian Medical Center in New York spent years studying the conflicting theories, using the experience and knowledge he gained as a military surgeon and the facilities of a noted medical research institution.

Using Mannlicher-Carcano rifles of the type Oswald owned, Dr. Lattimer fired hundreds of test rounds into "necks" and "bodies" he had formed out of fresh pork, which were meant to simulate human skin over human bones. His two sons, John, age seventeen, and Gary, fourteen, helped in the experiments. Both learned to fire the Mann-licher-Carcano with the same speed and accuracy displayed by Lee Harvey Oswald.

In his book, *Kennedy and Lincoln, Medical and Ballistic Comparisons of Their Assassinations*, Dr. Lattimer presented evidence to prove that Kennedy and Connally were struck by the same bullet. He concluded that Oswald was the lone assassin.

After the assassination, Jacqueline Kennedy, the president's widow, and his brother, Robert, asked historian William Manchester to inquire into the tragedy and write a book about it. Manchester spent three years on the project, questioning everyone that might be able to contribute information about the event. The list included members of the Secret Service, the physicians who performed the autopsy on the president's body, aides to Kennedy and President Lyndon Johnson, members of the Kennedy family, and the CIA and FBI. Manchester's book, *The Death of a President*, was published in 1967. In it, Manchester concluded Oswald was the president's killer and that he acted alone.

In more recent years, however, suspicions that Oswald was not the lone assassin have been fueled by other books and by Hollywood films. When the movie *JFK* was released in 1991, it triggered a new wave of controversy. The film declares that a vast web of political, government, and corporate interests were behind the killing. But many critics say the film is as fictional as *The Wizard of Oz*.

A poll conducted in 1992 by *Time* magazine and the Cable News Network reported that three quarters of Americans believe there was a conspiracy behind the assassination. The leading suspects are the CIA, the Mafia, the Cuban government, anti-Castro Cuban exiles, American military leaders, and the Dallas police.

Perhaps the truth about President Kennedy's assassination will never be known. Perhaps there was more than one gunman. Perhaps the president was the victim of an enormous conspiracy. But these are mere theories, and a theory is only an assumption or guess based on limited information or knowledge. Until believable evidence is presented to support any of the theories, it is fair to assume that Lee Harvey Oswald, acting alone, shot President John Kennedy.

9
Double Jeopardy

Is American society too gun-loving and trigger-happy to allow its political leaders to mix with its people?

That was the question being asked in the mid-1970s — and with good reason. One tragic shooting after another had jolted the nation.

Only five years after Kennedy had been assassinated, black civil rights leader Martin Luther King had gone to Memphis, Tennessee, in April 1968 in support of a strike by the city's sanitation workers. He was on the balcony of his room at the Lorraine Motel on April 4 when a lone assassin fired a bullet from a 30.06 caliber rifle that ripped into the right side of King's jaw, killing him.

On June 5 the same year, Robert Kennedy,

151

brother of the murdered president, and a candidate for the Democratic presidential nomination in 1968, was shot at a moment of personal triumph. He had won the California primary and had just finished delivering his victory speech at the Ambassador Hotel in Los Angeles. Bodyguards were leading him through the jubilant crowd when several shots rang out. One bullet entered the right side of Kennedy's head and proved fatal.

Four years later, on the afternoon of May 15, 1972, Alabama Governor George Wallace, running for the Democratic presidential nomination, was addressing an open air rally in Laurel, Maryland, when a gunman pumped four bullets into him. Wallace usually wore a bulletproof vest. But because the day was so hot, he had skipped it. One of the bullets lodged near Wallace's spinal column, leaving him paralyzed.

In 1975, the assassination menace flared again. This time the target was President Gerald Ford. Incredibly, not once, but twice in the space of seventeen days Ford found himself looking down the barrel of a pistol pointed at him.

Time magazine said the "assassin's disease" was spreading. Is there something wrong with American society? the magazine asked. Why does the nation seem to produce so many misfits willing to gun down people who hold positions of public importance?

No one seemed to have the answers.

*   *   *

Gerald Ford is the only vice president of the United States to have become president through the resignation of a chief executive. On August 8, 1974, Richard Nixon, facing almost certain impeachment for his role in the Watergate scandal, resigned as president, to be effective the next day. On August 9th, when Nixon left office, Ford took the oath as the nation's thirty-eighth president.

Ford had been vice president for only eight months before becoming president. Nixon had appointed Ford to replace Agnew, who had resigned while under investigation for corruption, leaving the position vacant.

Ford thus has the distinction of being the only person to serve as both vice president and president without ever having been elected to either office. He was, his wife, Betty, once noted, "an accidental vice president and an accidental president, and in both jobs he replaced disgraced leaders."

Ford enjoyed a long career as a congressman from Michigan before shifting to the executive branch of the government. He earned a reputation as a loyal Republican and hard worker. When President Lyndon Johnson set up the Warren Commission in 1963 to investigate the assassination of President Kennedy, he named Ford as one of the seven members of the commission. In the years after, Ford often spoke out in support of the commission's findings.

Sixty-one years old when he entered the White House, Ford, a former college football player, was in excellent physical shape. He was the most athletic president since Theodore Roosevelt. He enjoyed skiing, swimming, golf, and tennis.

Those who worked with Ford found him friendly and easy to get along with. A member of the Secret Service detail assigned to guard him once described Ford as "a nice guy trying to do his best in one of the most difficult jobs in the world."

In September 1975, Ford, who had then been president about thirteen months, traveled to the West Coast. One reason for the trip was to address the California state legislature in Sacramento. The subject of his talk: violent crime.

Ford arrived in Sacramento from Portland, Oregon, on the evening before his scheduled speech. He spent the night in a suite in the Senator Hotel in downtown Sacramento.

The next morning Ford addressed a breakfast gathering of more than a thousand of the area's leading citizens. They applauded enthusiastically when he attacked big government for its "cost, contradiction, and confusion."

After the breakfast meeting, Ford went back to the hotel. At five minutes to ten, right on schedule, he left the hotel on foot to walk a block to the state capitol. There he had a ten o'clock meeting with Governor Jerry Brown.

Ford liked to make as much personal contact with people as possible, to "press the flesh," as President Lyndon Johnson once put it. When he started across a small park in front of the capitol and was greeted by applause and cheers from a cluster of people who had been waiting to see him, Ford couldn't resist. Grinning, he plunged into the crowd.

A woman in a red dress was waiting for Ford. She was armed with a three-pound .45 caliber Colt automatic pistol.

Near a magnolia tree, Ford reached out to shake some hands. He was actually reaching for the hand of the woman in red. Then he froze. "I saw a hand coming up between several others in the front row," Ford would say later. "And obviously there was a gun in that hand."

The woman, no more than two feet from Ford at the time, cried out: "The country is a mess! This man is not your president!"

At that instant, a husky Secret Service agent, Larry Buendorf, lunged forward, wrestled the gun from the woman's grasp, and threw her to the ground. Other agents and police officers were suddenly on the scene to help Buendorf.

"Let's go!" another Secret Service agent shouted. That command was a signal to let the other agents know that Ford was in danger. Swiftly a wall of agents formed around the pale

Immediately after the attempt was made on President Ford's life in a park in Sacramento, California, he was grasped by Secret Service agents and rushed from the scene.

and shaken president to hurry him out of the park and into the safety of the capitol.

While the president was being whisked away, the woman in red continued to shout. "He's not a public servant!" she said. "He's not a public servant."

She also cried out: "It didn't go off! Can you believe it? It didn't go off!"

Why the gun didn't fire became clear when Secret Service agents examined it. The revolver was loaded with four bullets that were contained in a clip within the handle. But there was no bullet

Squeaky Fromme is wrestled to the ground after she pointed a gun at President Ford.

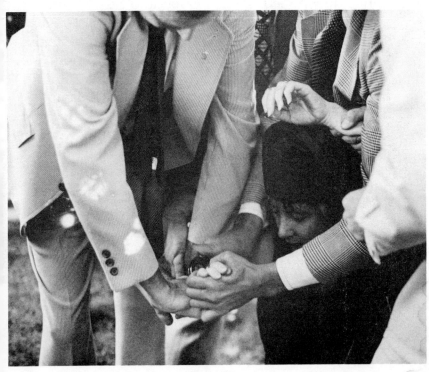

in the chamber ready to fire. In order to shoot, it was necessary to first pull back a slide at the top of the pistol, feeding a bullet from the clip into the chamber.

The woman who almost killed President Ford was Lynette Fromme. She was nicknamed Squeaky for her high-pitched little voice. Twenty-six years old, and a follower of Charles Manson, who was serving a life sentence as the leader of a murderous California cult, Squeaky was the first woman to attempt to kill a president of the United States.

In seeking to find out what made Squeaky Fromme want to kill the president, Sacramento police questioned Sandra Good and Susan Murphy, Fromme's two roommates. Sandra Good said that Fromme was "moved by the disaster facing the country from air and water pollution."

"Nixon lied to the people," said Good, "and Ford is continuing to lie to the people. He is not doing anything."

Good also said that she and Fromme were members of an international people's court that consisted of several thousand members throughout the world who were prepared to kill the polluters of air and water. She said: "We're going to start assassinating presidents, vice presidents, and major executives of companies. I'm warning these people they'd better stop polluting or they're going to die."

Speaking from her prison cell, Fromme herself

158

Squeaky Fromme being taken from federal court after being sentenced to life imprisonment.

said that she had sought to shoot the president because she "just wanted to get some attention for a new trial for Charlie [Manson] and the girls."

Asked why she had taken such drastic action, she replied: "Well, you know, when people around you treat you like a child and pay no attention to the things you say, you have to do something."

The attempted assassination of President Ford was not Fromme's first brush with the law. She had a long FBI record and had been arrested several times on charges ranging from drug possession to murder. However, she had been convicted only once, receiving a ninety-day sentence in 1971 for attempting to prevent a witness from testifying in a murder case.

In the months before the assassination attempt, Squeaky and her roommates had started wearing red robes. "Our red robes are an example of a new morality," she said. "We must clean up the air, water, and the land. They're red with sacrifice, the blood of sacrifice."

Squeaky Fromme's weird ways were not weird enough to qualify her as being insane. She was tried, found guilty of attempting to assassinate the president with a gun, and sentenced to life imprisonment.

President Ford took the attempt upon his life in stride. He didn't even mention it in his meeting with Governor Brown that morning and he went ahead as planned with his speech to the state legislature.

When he returned to Washington that night, Ford's wife greeted him with a bear hug. In reference to the assassination attempt, she said, "It's something you have to live with. I'm grateful to the Secret Service for the great job they do."

*   *   *

President Ford was back in California less than three weeks later, when he was again the victim of an assassination try. Some newspapers called it a "copycat act."

Ford arrived at San Francisco International Airport on September 21. The following day, as the presidential motorcade raced into town, spectators couldn't help but be impressed by the array of protection that was being provided. There were vehicles with Secret Service agents, highway patrolmen on motorcycles, military police, and county police. There was a SWAT (Special Weapons and Tactics) squad with rifles, furnished by San Mateo County. Every overpass was guarded by police with rifles. Security helicopters clattered overhead.

Ford's first stop in San Francisco was the Hyatt Hotel on Union Square. From there, he was to go to the St. Francis Hotel, also on the square. Even though it was an easy one-block walk, Ford made the trip in his limousine. The ride took less than half a minute. Secret Service agents jogged beside the car. Police with binoculars could be seen atop tall buildings that faced the square.

The president waved at the crowd as he hurried into the St. Francis for a reception that was to last for two or three hours. It was almost three-thirty in the afternoon before Ford was ready to leave. Across the street from the hotel, a large crowd had gathered.

When Ford came out of the hotel, he glanced to his right and left at small groups of spectators. As he walked toward his limousine, he saw the much larger crowd across the street. He smiled and paused. He seemed to be considering whether he should cross the street and shake some hands. Ford's Secret Service agents hoped he wouldn't. The memory of Squeaky Fromme was fresh in everyone's mind.

Then it happened. A pistol shot rang out. Ford stared straight across the street at the person holding the gun. He seemed dazed.

As Ford started to crouch, two Secret Service agents shoved him to the sidewalk. This placed Ford's car between him and the attacker. An agent opened the rear door of the limousine, and other agents practically threw Ford inside to the floor.

Two agents and Ford's Chief of Staff Donald Rumsfeld scrambled into the car with Ford. All three shielded Ford's body as the car sped away to the San Francisco airport and a rapid return to Washington.

Hearing the gunshot and watching Ford fall to the ground, many people in the crowd thought Ford had been shot. Some gasped; others screamed.

Two San Francisco policemen dove at Ford's would-be assassin, a heavy-set, middle-aged woman. One of them grabbed the cylinder of the .38 caliber revolver she held, preventing her from spinning another bullet into firing position. The other police officer grabbed her by the hair.

President Ford ducks outside Hotel St. Francis as a shot is fired.

The woman who fired at President Ford was Sara Jane Moore, forty-five, and, like Squeaky Fromme, a woman eager to pit herself against organized society. "It was kind of an ultimate protest against the system," Moore told a reporter from the Los Angeles *Times* in attempting to explain what she had done. "I did not want to kill somebody, but there comes a point when the only way you can make a statement is to pick up a gun. I was driven to act."

Sara Jane Moore pleaded guilty in the attempted assassination of President Ford and was sentenced to life imprisonment.

Moore came much closer to hitting the president than most people realized at first. When Ford came out of the hotel, Moore wasn't sure whether she could get a clear shot because there were so many people in front of her. She pulled the gun out, held it shoulder high with her right hand, and supported it with her left. "It was so easy, it was unbelievable," she said afterward.

Oliver Sipple, thirty-three, a former Marine and Vietnam veteran, was standing right beside Moore. When Ford waved, Sipple started to applaud. "At this point," he later said, "I saw this arm with the chrome-plated gun at the end of it." As Moore squeezed the trigger, the five-foot-eleven, 225-pound Sipple lunged toward her and grabbed her arm.

Sipple's leap may have saved Ford's life. "There's no question that he did deflect the weapon," said Lieutenant Frank Jordan of the San Francisco police. "Just as she shot, he pushed it aside. It was a very slight deflection, but it was enough."

As it was, the bullet didn't miss Ford by much. It passed within a few feet of him — five feet, said *Time* magazine — ricocheted away from the president and struck John Ludwig, an off-duty cab driver. Ludwig was not seriously hurt.

As in the case of most assassination attempts, no conspiracy was found. Sara Jane Moore acted alone.

Why had she sought to shoot President Ford? Her reasons were personal, not political. Earlier, she had been turned away by the FBI, for whom she once worked as an informant. She also had been shunned by many of her radical friends. Lonely and depressed, she perhaps had sought to relieve her sense of rejection by doing something startling.

Moore pleaded guilty to a charge of attempted assassination of the president. Like Squeaky Fromme, she was sentenced to a life in prison.

Following the second attempt on Ford's life, more than a few newspapers, television commentators, members of Congress, and experts on violence asked him to forsake his desire for personal contact with big crowds. Said columnist Joseph Kraft: "Mr. Ford is in effect baring his chest, sticking out his chin, and daring every kook in the country to take a shot at him."

But the attempts on his life didn't make Ford any more cautious. In the presidential primaries in 1976 and in the campaign for the presidency that fall, Ford did not hesitate to greet well wishers — shaking hands, posing for photographs, and signing autographs.

Ford was narrowly defeated by Jimmy Carter in the election of 1976. Since leaving the White House, he has spent much of his time before the public, often lecturing at colleges and universities, and speaking to organizations. Never again has he had to stare down the barrel of an assassin's gun.

10
Close Call

Monday, March 30, 1981, began as a routine day for Ronald Reagan. Around eight forty-five that morning, the president entered the Oval Office for a briefing with his top aides, mainly his chief of staff and national security adviser. He was wearing a brand new blue pinstripe suit for a speech early in the afternoon at the Washington Hilton Hotel to 3,500 delegates attending a union convention.

Elected in 1980, the sixty-nine-year-old president had been inaugurated only seventy days before. The "Reagan Revolution," as one of his aides called it, had scarcely begun. The new president had proposed big tax cuts along with reductions in welfare and unemployment programs. He had also asked for large increases in defense spending. But Congress had yet to act on the president's proposals.

When it came time to leave for the Hilton, a five-minute drive from the White House, Reagan decided against wearing a bulletproof vest. He didn't think his "iron underwear," as he called it, would be necessary, because his only exposure to the public would be a thirty-foot walk to his limousine.

At about the same time the president was getting ready to leave for the hotel, a twenty-five-year-old drifter from Evergreen, Colorado, John W. Hinckley, sat down in his room at the Park Central Hotel in Washington, two blocks from the White House, to write a love letter. It was addressed to Jodie Foster, an 18-year-old movie star who played the role of a teenage prostitute in the film *Taxi Driver*. The movie starred Robert De Niro as a crazed gunman who plans to kill a presidential candidate.

In part, Hinckley's letter read:

Dear Jodie:

There is a definite possibility I will be killed in my attempt to get Reagan. It is for this very reason that I am writing you now.

As you well know by now, I love you very much. The past seven months I have left you dozens of poems, letters and messages in the faint hope you would develop an interest in me.

Although we talked on the phone a couple of times, I never had the nerve to simply approach you and introduce myself. Besides my shyness, I honestly do not wish to bother you . . . I know that the many messages left at your door were a nuisance, but I felt it was the most painless way for me to express my love to you.

Jodie, I would abandon this idea of getting

Hinckley said he was seeking to impress Jodie Foster, who played the role of a prostitute in the movie Taxi Driver.

Reagan in a second if I could only win your heart and live out the rest of my life with you, whether it be in total obscurity or whatever, I will admit to you the reason I am going ahead with this attempt now is because I just cannot wait any longer to impress you.

Jodie, I'm asking you to please look into your heart and at least give me the chance with this historical deed to gain your love.

I love you forever.

(signed) John Hinckley

Shortly after finishing the letter, Hinckley set out for the Washington Hilton. With him he carried a six-shot snub-nosed .22 caliber pistol, a weapon often described as a "Saturday night special." The type of bullet he carried was vicious. Known as the Devastator, each bullet would explode on impact.

After he arrived at the Hilton, Hinckley noticed that reporters and television cameras were clustered behind a red-velvet rope outside the hotel's VIP entrance. They were planning to cover the president when he entered the hotel and later made his exit. No one seemed to mind that a number of spectators had crowded in behind the reporters and TV crews. Hinckley joined the fifteen to twenty onlookers.

Reagan received a standing ovation when he arrived at the ballroom of the Hilton to deliver his speech, and it went off without a hitch. After speaking, he left the ballroom to go to a "holding room" before leaving the hotel. There he spoke with his aides and met dignitaries. At the same time, Secret Service agents and other security people were making their way from the ballroom to the driveway outside the VIP entrance.

As the president left the hotel, the spectators who had been waiting cheered and clapped. Several reporters and TV cameramen called out, "Mr. President! Over here, Mr. President!" Reagan grinned and raised his right arm.

At that instant, Hinckley pulled out his gun, dropped to a crouch and, using a cop's two-handed grip, started firing. It sounded like firecrackers — *Pop! Pop! Pop!*

Reagan turned and said, "What the hell's that?"

Jerry Parr, the head of the Secret Service detail, knew what it was. He grabbed Reagan by the waist and hurled him into the backseat of the limousine, then piled in on top of him. Reagan landed on his face, atop an armrest.

The president felt intense pain in his upper back, the worst pain he had ever felt in his life. "Jerry," he screamed, "get off; I think you've broken one of my ribs."

"The White House!" Jerry told the driver. As the car roared away, Reagan tried to sit up but was almost paralyzed by the pain. Then he started coughing up blood.

"You not only broke a rib," Reagan said, look-

Shaken and wounded, the president is shoved into his car by Secret Service agents.

ing at his blood-stained handkerchief, "I think the rib punctured my lung." Jerry saw the blood and ordered the driver to head for George Washington University Hospital instead of the White House.

Hinckley had fired six times, pulling the trigger as fast as he could. Just as the last bullet left his gun, he was flattened by a Secret Service agent. Other agents piled on top of the two men. Handcuffs were quickly snapped on Hinckley, who made no effort to resist.

As the agents got Hinckley to his feet, a man lunged for him from the crowd of spectators, and managed to get his hands around Hinckley's throat. Secret Service agents knocked the man away.

The agents were screaming commands at one another. The bodies of three men were on the ground. James Brady, the president's press secretary, was face down, bleeding from a wound in his head. Thomas Delahanty, a District of Columbia policeman, lay on the ground, moaning in pain. Secret Service agent Timothy McCarthy, also struck by one of Hinckley's bullets, lay silent.

Besides Reagan, Hinckley's attack left three others wounded, including officer Thomas Delehanty (foreground) and presidential press secretary James Brady (behind Delehanty).

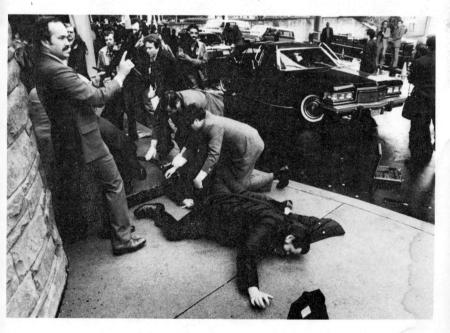

As his limousine sped to the hospital, Reagan began to have trouble breathing. "I felt like a hammer had hit me," he said later.

The limousine streaked into the emergency entrance of the hospital, arriving just three minutes after the shooting. Reagan got out of the car and started walking toward the emergency room. A nurse came to meet him. He told her he was having difficulty breathing. Suddenly, he staggered and his knees began to buckle. Two Secret Service agents grabbed him. "I can't breathe," he whispered.

Reagan was lifted onto a wheeled table and the emergency crew went to work on him. The last thing he remembered before passing out was that his brand new blue pinstripe suit was being cut off of him, and he would never be able to wear it again.

It didn't take doctors long to determine that Reagan had been shot. A bullet from Hinckley's gun had ricocheted off the car's armored door, torn into his body under the left arm, bounced off a rib, and punctured his left lung. It had come to rest only three inches from his heart.

In x-rays, the bullet showed up as a small white spot in the left lung. It had left a three-inch tear in the lung, which continued to bleed.

Doctors decided to operate immediately to remove the bullet and stop the bleeding. When surgeons located the bullet, they found it had flattened to the size of a nickel from the impact

"All the News That's Fit to Print"

The New York Times

LATE CITY EDITION

Weather: Mostly sunny, mild today, fair tonight. Chance of showers tomorrow. Temperature range: today 66-42; yesterday 56-33. Details on page C1.

VOL.CXXX..No. 44,904

NEW YORK, TUESDAY, MARCH 31, 1981

25 CENTS

REAGAN WOUNDED IN CHEST BY GUNMAN; OUTLOOK 'GOOD' AFTER 2-HOUR SURGERY; AIDE AND 2 GUARDS SHOT; SUSPECT HELD

Bush Flies Back From Texas Set to Take Charge in Crisis

By STEVEN R. WEISMAN
Special to The New York Times

WASHINGTON, March 30 — Vice President Bush, cutting short a trip to Texas, returned to the White House this evening to take charge of the crisis in the Government and to assume the responsibilities of the Presidency if President Reagan's injuries prevented him from serving in the office.

It was unclear tonight how long Mr. Bush would remain in charge of Government functions, however. At George Washington University Hospital, the dean of clinical affairs said that President Reagan was "alert" and that he "should be able to make decisions by tomorrow."

But he would have to remain in the hospital for two weeks.

"I can reassure this nation and a watching world that the American Government is functioning fully and effectively," Mr. Bush said this evening after presiding over a half-hour Cabinet meeting in the White House situation room, where participants also heard the televised news conference reporting on Mr. Reagan's condition.

'Officers Fulfilling Obligations'

"We've had full and complete communications throughout the day, and the officers of the Federal Government have been fulfilling their obligations with skill and with care," Mr. Bush continued. He added that "all our prayers" and "all our hope" were extended for the recovery of the two wounded law enforcement men and for James S. Brady, the White House press secretary.

White House spokesmen said this evening that no steps had been taken to install Mr. Bush as Acting President under the terms of the 25th Amendment to the Constitution, which provides for succession in case of Presidential disability.

Mr. Bush was scheduled to sit in for the President tomorrow, however, at a series of previously scheduled functions, including a Cabinet meeting, a session with Congressional leaders, and a lunch with the Prime Minister of the Netherlands, Andreas A. M. van Agt. He prepared to

Americans were saddened and outraged by news of the shooting of the President. In the business community, activity came to a standstill; stock trading was halted. Pages A1 and D1.

spend the night at his own official residence in northwest Washington, a few miles from the White House.

Contradictory Statements

There were contradictory statements in the afternoon and evening about who was in charge of the Government.

Shortly after 4 P.M., Secretary of State Alexander M. Haig Jr., who rushed to the White House minutes after the attack, announced he was in control pending the return of the Vice President to Washington. Mr. Haig also said he was in charge because the newly created system of "crisis management" was in effect, and he suggested that it was his role to serve as crisis-management coordinator until the

Continued on Page A3, Column 2

Suspect Was Arrested Last Year In Nashville on Weapons Charge

By PHILIP TAUBMAN
Special to The New York Times

WASHINGTON, Tuesday, March 31 — The 25-year-old son of a Denver oil executive was surrendered by police officers and Secret Service agents yesterday at the scene of an attack on President Reagan. He was charged with the attempted assassination of the President and the shooting of three other persons.

The suspect was identified as John W. Hinckley Jr., who was said to have been in psychiatric care recently. He was arrested in Nashville last Oct. 9 for possession of concealed weapons, according to Nashville police records, and was released after paying a fine of $62.50. President Carter had arrived in Nashville a few hours earlier that night to speak at Opry Land.

Yesterday, in the tumult that followed the firing of a series of shots at Mr. Reagan's party, Mr. Hinckley was grabbed and pushed against a wall outside the Washington Hilton Hotel. Secret Service agents said that a Harrington Richardson .22-caliber pistol was recovered from him, and he was quickly taken away in a District of Columbia police car.

Mr. Hinckley, described as a blue-eyed, sandy-haired man about 5 feet 10 inches tall, was turned over by police to the Federal Magistrate Arthur L. Burnett on a charge that he "knowingly and intentionally" attempted to kill President Reagan and assaulted a Secret Service

Continued on Page A4, Column 4

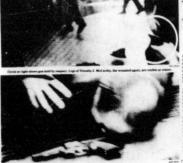

John W. Hinckley Jr. in photo made Jan. 22 for his driver's license.

Witnesses to Shooting Recall Suspect Acting 'Fidgety' and 'Hostile'

By RICHARD D. LYONS
Special to The New York Times

WASHINGTON, March 30 — "I spotted him smirking rapidly up and down outside the back door of the hotel," John W. Dodson said. "He looked fidgety — agitated — a little strange, and I said to myself 'Aha,' if he takes a shot at the President?"

Mr. Dodson, a computer specialist, was not the only person to take note of the behavior of the blond young man outside the Washington Hilton where President Reagan was making a speech. Walter C. Rogers, a reporter for Associated Press Radio, said the young man had been hostile to the group of reporters he had penetrated. And another witness, Samuel Lofta, an iron worker from Warren, Mich. said that a police lieutenant had stared at the young man several times.

But nothing was done until the shots that wounded the President, his press secretary and two guards rang out. Then, the young man was overwhelmed by police officers and Secret Service agents.

Mr. Dodson, who works for U.S. Pinkerton Detective Agency was standing on the seventh floor of the Universal North

Continued on Page A3, Column 2

Other News

Polish Strike Suspended

A nationwide strike threatened for today was averted after leaders of Solidarity reached a tentative settlement with the Polish Government. Page A9.

Indonesians Storm Hijacked Jet

Four of five hijackers were slain and 55 hostages freed when commandos in Bangkok stormed an Indonesian airliner held since Saturday. Page A4.

National News A16	Music C14
Books C20	Notes on People ... B6
Bridge C20	Obituaries B10
Business Day D1,D2	Op-Ed A31
Chess C20	Science Times C1
Crossword C20	Shipping D12
Dance C14	Sports B8-13
Editorials A30	Style A20
Education C4	Theaters C9
Going Out Guide C7	TV/Radio C18
Letters A30	U.N. Events A4
Man in the News A16	Weather C1

News Summary and Index, Page B1

FOR HOME DELIVERY OF THE NEW YORK TIMES
Call toll free 800-631-2500. In N.J. 800-242-8208.

President Reagan leaving the Washington Hilton. At right is James S. Brady. As Mr. Reagan waved to the crowd...

...the gunman fired, hitting the President below his left arm. In photo made over roof of Presidential car...

...Secret Service agents are seen pushing Mr. Reagan into the vehicle, which immediately sped to a hospital.

Circle at right shows gun held by suspect. Logo of Timothy J. McCarthy, the wounded agent, are visible at center.

James S. Brady lies on sidewalk. The pistol is believed to belong to a security agent, who put it down while helping.

LEFT LUNG IS PIERCED

Coloradan, 25, Arrested — Brady, Press Chief, Is Critically Injured

By HOWELL RAINES
Special to The New York Times

WASHINGTON, Tuesday, March 31 — President Reagan was shot in the chest yesterday by a gunman, apparently acting alone, as Mr. Reagan walked to his limousine after addressing a labor meeting at the Washington Hilton Hotel. The White House press secretary and two law-enforcement officers were also wounded by a burst of shots.

The President was reported in "good" and "stable" condition last night at George Washington University Hospital.

Statements in critical, pages A1 and A7.

after undergoing two hours of surgery. "The prognosis is excellent," said Dr. Dennis S. O'Leary, dean of clinical affairs at the university. "He is alert and should be able to make decisions by tomorrow."

The hospital spokesman said surgeons removed a .22-caliber bullet that struck Mr. Reagan's seventh rib, penetrating the left lung three inches and collapsing it.

A rapid series of five or six shots rang out about 2:30 P.M. as Mr. Reagan left the hotel. A look of stunned disbelief swept across the President's face when the shots were fired just after he raised his left arm to wave to the crowd. Nearby, his press secretary, James S. Brady, fell to the sidewalk, critically wounded.

Eyewitnesses said six shots were fired at the Presidential entourage from a distance of about 10 feet. The assailant had positioned himself among the television camera crews and reporters assembled outside a hotel exit.

The authorities arrested a 25-year-old Colorado man, John W. Hinckley Jr., at the scene of the attack. He was booked on Federal charges of attempting to assassinate the President and assault on a Federal officer, and early this morning he was ordered held without bail by Federal Magistrate Arthur L. Burnett.

According to police records, Mr. Hinckley was arrested in Nashville last fall on weapons charges on a night when President Carter was speaking there.

Scene of Turmoil

Within moments after the attack yesterday afternoon, Americans were witnessing for the second time in a generation television pictures of a chief executive being struck by gunfire during what appeared to be a routine public appearance. For the second time in less than 20 years, too, they watched as the nation's leaders scrambled to meet one of the severest tests of the democratic system.

Mr. Reagan, apparently at first unaware that he had been wounded, was shoved forcefully by a Secret Service agent into the Presidential limousine,

Continued on Page A3, Column 1

A Bullet Is Removed From Reagan's Lung In Emergency Surgery

By ROBERT REINHOLD
Special to The New York Times

WASHINGTON, March 30 — President Reagan was treated for a partly collapsed lung today, but the bullet that entered his left side and lodged in the tissue of his left lung did not do much further damage, according to doctors who operated on him. Surgeons removed a .22-caliber bullet from the President's lower left lung.

Neither Mr. Reagan's heart nor such vital blood vessels as the aorta were affected, Dr. Dennis S. O'Leary, dean for clinical affairs at George Washington University, said in a brief report this evening. "The bullet was never close to any vital structure," he said. He called Mr. Reagan's prognosis "excellent."

Emergency surgical procedures, which took about two hours, found no bleeding or damage in the abdominal area. Mr. Reagan received five units, or two and a half quarts, of blood in a transfusion before surgery. His vital signs were stable throughout his ordeal.

The aide said the bullet that entered relates to how rapidly the blood is lost and whether the volume of the blood sup-

Continued on Page A7, Column 1

with the door of the president's armored car. A surgeon removed the bullet with a probe and handed it to a Secret Service agent. Surgeons then repaired the tear in the president's lung and closed the incision.

Reagan made a speedy recovery. Twelve days later, he was back in the White House, although he was not anywhere near ready to resume his normal schedule. A six-inch scar on his chest was a reminder of how close he had come to sudden death.

The wounded Thomas Delahanty and Timothy McCarthy also recovered. The brain-injured James Brady, however, was hospitalized for months, and never regained full use of his body.

John Hinckley did not hate Ronald Reagan. He had nothing against his policies. He shot the president in an attempt to impress the young movie actress Jodie Foster.

When Hinckley was brought into court for the first time and cited for attempting to kill the president, he was asked if he understood the charges. "Yes, sir," he said softly.

Did he have a job? "No, sir," he said.

Any dependents? "No, sir."

Could he afford to pay a lawyer? "No, sir." The judge appointed two court lawyers to defend him.

During the courtroom proceedings, it was revealed that Hinckley had a history of following presidents around. On October 9, 1980, he had

John Hinckley, a twenty-five-year-old drifter from Evergreen, Colorado, acting alone, shot Reagan and three others in the assassination attempt.

been arrested at the airport in Nashville, Tennessee, when X-ray equipment disclosed he had three handguns and ammunition in his carry-on bag. President Carter was in Nashville that day. Hinckley was fined $62.50 and the guns were taken from him.

Four days later, Hinckley turned up in Dallas. There he bought two .22 caliber handguns at Rocky's Pawn Shop on East Elm Street, not far from where President Kennedy had been shot. One of these guns was used in the attack on President Reagan.

It was later learned that Hinckley was the son of a wealthy oil executive. He had grown up in Highland Park, a comfortable suburb of Dallas, Texas. The Hinckleys lived in Highland Park from 1966 to 1974, when the family moved to Colorado. John was an average student, an average athlete.

Hinckley attended Texas Tech University on an off-and-on basis, never graduating. He made frequent trips across the country and in 1978 joined the National Socialist Party of America, usually called the Nazi Party. After the attempt on President Reagan's life, a spokesperson for the Party said Hinckley had not had his membership renewed because of his "violent temper."

Sometime in 1980, Hinckley began his fantasy romance with actress Jodie Foster. At the time, she was a student at Yale University in New Haven, Connecticut.

Hinckley went to New Haven, perhaps with the idea of meeting Foster. The FBI recovered a letter in Hinckley's hotel room in Washington addressed to Foster but never mailed. It read: "Although we talked on the phone a couple of times, I never had the nerve to simply approach you and introduce myself." Foster said she had "never met, spoken to, or in any way associated with Hinckley."

In 1982, a jury found Hinckley to be insane at the time of the assassination attempt. He was therefore found not guilty of the attempted murder charge. A federal judge later ordered that

One of Hinckley's letters to Jodie Foster, used as evidence in his trial.

Hinckley be placed in a mental institution. Since then, he has been confined to St. Elizabeth's Hospital in Washington, D.C.

In the years following the assassination attempt, James Brady and his wife have become very active in seeking gun control legislation. They work hard for the passage of a bill that would require a seven-day waiting period between the purchase and delivery of a handgun.

Called the "Brady Bill," it could help to frustrate the smuggling of guns from states with lax gun laws to states with strong ones.

Ronald Reagan, as president, always opposed gun-control legislation. But after visiting Brady on March 30, 1991, the tenth anniversary of Hinckley's attack, Reagan said he had undergone a change of heart, and he called upon Congress to enact the Brady Bill.

Index

Italics indicate illustrations

A

Agnew, Spiro, 153
American Samoa, 56
Anarchism, 57–58, 59, 61, 67
Antisemitism, 125
Arthur, Chester A., 41, 47, 49, 50
Assassination attempts, numbers of, in U.S., 1–2
Assassins, personalities of, 2. *See also entries under names of individual assassins*
Astor, Vincent, 86–87
Atzerodt, George, 31

B

Barnes, Joseph K., 47–48
Baudouin (K. of Belgium), 143
Bell, Alexander Graham, 48
Berlin, Germany, 124
Birdzell, Donald, 110, 111, 113, 115

Blaine, James G., 37, 40–41, 43, 44
Blair, Francis Preston, 107
Blair, Montgomery, 107
Blair House, 102–103, 104, 107, *112*, *114*
Booth, Edwin, 24
Booth, John Wilkes, *23*, *29*; assassination of Lincoln by, 25–30; biography of, 23–24; death of, 31, 33; escape of, 30; hunt for, 31; personal description of, 22; plots of, 22–23, 24–25; rewards for capture of, *32*
Booth, Junius, 24
Boring, Floyd, 110–111
Brady, James, 173, 176, 179
Brady, Sarah, 179
Bresci, Gaetano, 61
Brown, Jerry, 155, 160
Bryan, William Jennings, 56

181

Buendorf, Larry, 155
Buffalo, New York, 53, 70
Bull Moose Party (Progressive
  Party), 73, 75
Burns, Francis, 22

C

Cabell, Mrs. Earle, 135
Campos, Pedro, 106
Capone, Al, 101
Carter, Jimmy, 117–118, 166,
  177
Castro, Fidel, 123
Central Intelligence Agency (CIA),
  123, 146, 147, 149, 150
Cermak, Anton J., 94–95, 96, 97–
  98, 100, 101
Channing, Walter, 60
Chickamauga, Battle of, 37
Civil Service Commission (U.S.),
  41, 50
Civil War (U.S.): Booth, John
  Wiles and, 23, 24; celebration at
  ending of, 13; Garfield, James
  and, 37; McKinley, William
  and, 55
Coffelt, Leslie, 110, 111–112, 113,
  115, 116, 117
Collazo, Oscar: assassination at-
  tempt by, 104–105, 106–114;
  biography of, 105, 106; commu-
  tation of sentence of, 117–118;
  trial of 115–117
Connally, John, 128, 130, 133, 135,
  148, 149
Constitution (U.S.), Presidential
  term limitations, 85
Corbett, Boston, 31
Cortelyou, George, 63
Crook, William, 17, 18, 19
Cross, Lillian, 95–96, 96, 97
Cuba, 123, 124, 150
Curry, Jesse, 130
Czolgosz, Leon F., 57, 75; assassination motive of, 56–58, 67–68,
  69; assassination of McKinley
  by, 64, 65, 66; assassination plot
  of, 55, 62–64; biography of, 58–

62; execution of, 69; trial of,
  68

D

Dallas, Texas, 125, 150
Davidson, Joseph, 110–111
Davis, Warren R., 5, 8
Delahanty, Thomas, 173, 176
Dill, John, 194
Donovan, Robert J., 100
Downs, Joseph, 111, 113, 115

E

Eckert, Thomas T., 17–18
Edison, Thomas, 53
Electric lights, 53
Euins, Amos Lee, 136

F

Federal Bureau of Investigation
  (FBI), 149; Fromme, Lynette
  and, 160; Oswald, Lee Harvey
  and, 123–124, 139; Warren
  Commission and, 146
Flammang, Anna, 75, 76
Flammang, Dominick, 75, 76
Forbes, Charles, 22
Ford, Betty, 153, 160
Ford, Gerald: assassination at-
  tempts on, 152, 154–155, 156,
  157, 157–162, 163, 163–166;
  sworn in as President, 153
Ford, Harry, 15
Ford's Theatre, 14, 15, 16, 24, 25,
  30, 34, 43
Foster, Jodie, 168–169, 169, 170,
  176, 178
Frazier, Wesley, 126, 127
Frederika (Q. of Greece), 143
Fromme, Lynette "Squeaky," 163;
  assassination attempt by, 157,
  157–158, 159, 159–160, 162; as-
  sassination motive of, 158–159;
  sentence of, 160

G

Garfield, James, 36, 50; assassination of, 2, 35, 45, 46, 46, 102;

182

assassination plot against, 37–
38, 41–45; biography of, 36–37;
death of, 49; funeral of, 49–50;
Guiteau, Charles and, 39–40;
injuries to, 47–49
Gaulle, Charles de, 143
Goldman, Emma, 61
Good, Sandra, 158
Grant, Ulysses S., 13, 14, 15, 19–
20, 37, 39
Great Depression, 91, 92
Guam, 56
Guiteau, Charles, *38*; appearance
of, 38; assassination plot of, 41–
45; diplomatic post sought by,
39–41; execution of, 51–52, *52*;
Garfield assassinated by, 45, 46,
46; trial of, 50–51
Guns: assassinations and, 2–3;
laws controlling, 179–180

H

Hancock, Winfield Scott, 37, 39
Handguns. *See* Guns
Harris, Clara, 20, 21–22, 30
Harris, Ira, 20
Hawaii, 56
Herold, David, 31
Hill, Clint, 135
Hinckley, John W., *177*; assassina-
tion attempt by, 170–176, *177*;
assassination motivation of,
176; biography of, 178; commit-
ment to mental institution of,
178–179; guns and, 176–177;
mental state of, 168–170
Hoover, Herbert, 86, 92, 93

J

Jackson, Andrew, *5*, 73, 107; assassination attempt on, 4–5, 8–
10, *10*; belief of, regarding assassination attempt, 11–12
Jackson, Bob, 136
Japan, 2, 72
Jefferson, Thomas, 73
Johnson, Andrew, 23, 25, 31,
34

Johnson, Lyndon B., 121, 124,
125, 130, 143, 149, 153, 155;
sworn in as President, 135, *136*;
Warren Commission established
by, 146
Jordon, Frank, 165

K

Kearney, Patrick, 46
Keene, Laura, 14, 21
Kennedy, Caroline, *120*, 121, 141,
143
Kennedy, Jacqueline, 121, 127–
128, 130, 131, 133, 135, 141,
143, 149
Kennedy, John F., 70, *120*; assassination of, 2, 119–121, 128–
134, *134*, 135, *142*, 151, 177; assassination plot against, 126–
127; controversy surrounding
assassination of, 145–150; election of, 124; funeral of, 141, 143,
144, *145*; injuries to, 133, 134–
135; Texas trip of, 124–126,
127–128, *129*
Kennedy, John F., Jr., *120*, 121,
141, 143
Kennedy, Robert, 143, 149; assassination of, 3, 151–152
King, Martin Luther, Jr., assassination of, 3, 151
Korean War, 104, 117
Kosciusko, Thaddeus, 76
Kraft, Joseph, 165–166

L

Lattimer, John K., 148–149
Lawrence, Richard: assassination
attempt by, 9–10, *10*; commitment to insane asylum, 11;
mental state of, 6–8; trial of, 10
Leale, Charles, 30–31
Lee, Robert E., 13
Lincoln, Abraham, 13, *14*, 15, 21–
22, 37, 48, 107; assassination of,
2, 28–30, 35, 43, 56, 102; Booth,
John Wilkes and, 24; death of,
31; funeral of, *33*; guest list of,

183

Lincoln, Abraham (*cont.*)
19–20; premonition of assassination, 17, 19; trial of assassins of, 33–34
Lincoln, Mary Todd, 14, 15, 16, 17, 20, 21–22, 28, 29
Lincoln, Robert T., 14, 47
Lincoln, Tad, 13
Lovell, Joseph, 107
Lubke, Heinrich, 143
Ludwig, John, 165
Lyle, John H., 100

M

Mafia, 100–101, 123, 147, 150
Manchester, William, 149
Manson, Charles, 158, 159
McCarthy, Timothy, 173, 176
McDonald, M. N., 138
McKinley, William, 74–75, 77, 85; assassination of, 2, 64, *65*, *66*, *68*, 70, 102; assassination plot against, 62–64; biography of, 55–56; Buffalo, N.Y., visit of, 53–54, *54*; death of, 67; injuries to, 66–67
Middle East, assassinations in, 2
Milburn, John G., 63, 67
Moore, Sara Jane: assassination attempt by, 163, *164*, 164–165; assassination motive of, 165; sentence of, 165
Mroz, Vincent, 111
Mudd, Samuel, 31
Murphy, Susan, 158

N

Nationalist Party (Puerto Rico), 105–106, 115
New Orleans, Battle of, 4
Nitti, Frank, 101
Nixon, Richard, 124, 153
Nobel Peace Prize, 72

O

O'Donnell, Kenny, 119
Oswald, Lee Harvey, *122*; arrest of, 138–139; assassination motive of, 123; assassination of Kennedy by, 130, 132, 133, 135, 150; assassination plot of, 126–127; biography of, 121–123; case against, 139–140; conspiracy theories and, 145–146, 147, 148, 149; death of, 140–141, escape of, 137–138
Oswald, Marina, 123, 139
Our American Cousin (play), 14, 21

P

Paine, Lewis, 31, 44
Paine, Ruth, 126–127
Panama Canal, 72
Pan-American Exposition (Buffalo, N.Y., 1901), 53, 62, 63
Parker, John F., 17, 18–19, 20–21, 22, 33
Parr, Jerry, 171
Persian Gulf War (1991), 56
Philippines, 56
Poland, 58, 76
Police forces, Presidential protection and, 17, 18
Politics: Garfield, James and, 37, 39, 41; Jackson, Andrew and, 11; Korean War and, 104; McKinley, William and, 56; Presidential term limitations, 85; Puerto Rico and, 105–106; Roosevelt, Theodore and, 72–74; Schrank, John N. and, 76, 77
Progressive Party (Bull Moose Party), 73, 75
Puerto Rico, 56, 194; economic conditions in, 116; politics and, 105, 115; Truman, Harry and, 116–117

R

Rathbone, Henry Reed, 20, 21, 28, 30
Reagan, Ronald: assassination attempt on, 168, 170–171, *172*, 172–174, *175*, 176; gun control supported by, 180; injuries to,

174, 176; program of, 167–168
Reconstruction, 16
Roosevelt, Franklin D., 85, *87*, *95*, 102; assassination attempt on, 86–88, 93–97; assassination plot against, 93
Roosevelt, Theodore, 56, *71*, 154; assassination attempt on, 80–81, *81*, 82, *82*, 83; assassination plot against, 73, 74, *74*, 75, 78–80; becomes President, 67, *68*, 70; biography of, 70–72; injuries to, 81, 83, *83*, 84; politics and, 72–74
Ruby, Jack, 140, 141, 147
Rumsfeld, Donald, 162
Russia, 72. *See also* Soviet Union

S
Samoa, 56
Schrank, John N.: assassination attempt by, 80–81; assassination motive of, 74–75, 77–78; assassination plot of, 73, 74, *74*, 75, 78–80; biography of, 75–77; commitment to insane asylum, 84–85; mental state of, 84
Secret Service (U.S.), 17, 64, 87, 94, 97, 105, 110–111, 113–114, 125, 128, 130, 131, 146, 149, 154, 155, 160, 161, 162, 171, 172
Selassie, Haile (E. of Ethiopia), 143
Seward, William, 23, 25, 31, 43
Seward, William T., 47
Sipple, Oliver, 164–165
Slavery, Booth, John Wilkes and, 23
Sousa, John Philip, 53
Soviet Union, 123, 124. *See also* Russia
Spanish-American War, 56, 72, 115
Stalwarts (Republican faction), 41
Stanton, Edwin, 17–18
Stevenson, Adlai, 125

T
Taft, William Howard, 73, 84
Texas School Book Depository, 121–122, 123, 126, 127, 129–130, 131–132, 136, 137, 146
Tippit, J. D., 137–138, 139–140
Torresola, Doris, 105–106
Torresola, Griselio: assassination attempt by, 104–105, 106–114; biography of, 105–106
Trenchard, Asa, 27, 28
Truly, Roy, 137
Truman, Harry, *103*; assassination attempt on, 1, 102, 103–105, 106–114; Puerto Rico and, 116–117

U
Umberto I (K. of Italy), 61, 62–63
United States Treasury Guards, 15

V
Victor Emmanuel III (K. of Italy), 88, 90

W
Wallace, George, assassination attempt on, 152
War of 1812, 4
Warren Commission and Report, 153; criticism of, 145–148; establishment of, 146
Washington, George, 73, 76
Whig Party, 11
White House, 1, 102
Wilson, Woodrow, elected President, 84
Woodbury, Levi, 9

Z
Zangara, Giuseppe: assassination attempt of, 88, 93–97; biography of, 88–91; capture of, *98*; execution of, 99; imprisonment of, *89*; mental state of, 86, 99–100; trial of, 98–100